# "I'd Swap My Old Skidoo For You"

On the coast of Alaska rises a mountain named Susitna. It is known by locals as the "Sleeping Lady." The rounded, snow-covered summit and flanks are shaped like a woman in repose. Her hair drifts into the waters of Cook Inlet.

Legend says when the Sleeping Lady wakes up, there will be peace in the world.

One grumpy old sourdough who survived the Great Alaska Earthquake of 1964 says, "If that sweet lady ever wakes up, there's gonna be a whole lot of shaking going on. It'll be one hell of an earthquake."

To the east of The Lady is Nancy Lake and a whistle stop in the wilderness known as Willow.

There, a madcap old homesteader sings about his Lady of Susitna. As the northern lights twinkle in the starry winter nights, strains of John Hale's whiskey gravel voice and strumming guitar can be heard over the Saturday evening mirth at a tumbled down old bar in the swamp known as the Willow Trading Post.

I drove a herd of caribou
That was my fondest boast
That's how I came to be
At the Willow Trading Post
I met a girl from Nancy Lake
Her eyes were big and blue
I asked her what her name was
She said, "Susitna Sue."

Susitna Sue, Susitna Sue
Her hair is brown
Her eyes are blue
I'd swap my old skidoo for you!
Susitna Sue, Susitna Sue
There ain't no gal as true
As my sweet Susitna Sue.

# "I'd Swap My Old Skidoo For You"

## A Portrait Of Characters On The Last Frontier

## Nan Elliot

Sammamish Press
Issaquah, Washington

*For those who do not live in snow country and may be baffled by the title, a "skidoo" is the name Alaskans commonly use for a snowmobile. Snowmobiles are a major form of transportation in the wilderness of Alaska.*

Grateful acknowledgement is made to John Hale for the lyrics of his song and to ski-doo for use of its name, which in Alaska is synonymous with nearly every snow machine.

*Library of Congress Cataloging-in-Publication Data*

Elliot, Nan.
      I'd swap my old skidoo for you: a portrait of characters on the
last frontier / by Nan Elliot.
        p.     cm.
     ISBN 0-942381-06-8: $19.95 (softbound)
     ISBN 0-942381-07-6: $34.95 (hardbound)
     1. Alaska—Biography.     2. Pioneers—Alaska—Biography.
3. Frontier and pioneer life—Alaska.    4. Alaska—Social life and
customs.    I. Title
CT222.E45     1989
979.8'00992—dc20
  [B]                                                      89-28127
                                                        CIP

First printing 1989
Printed in Salt Lake City, Utah, by Publishers Press, Inc.

Cover photo of famous musher Joe Redington, Sr., and Mt. McKinley by Jeff Schultz.
Title page photo of John Hale by Dennis Hellawell.

Design and production by Laing Communications Inc., Bellevue, Washington.
    Editorial coordination—Ina Chang
    Design and layout—Sandra J. Harner
    Production coordination—Candice Duncan Cross
    Editorial and production support—Anita Hardy

Distributed in the United States by
    Sammamish Press
    P.O. Box 895
    Issaquah, Washington 98027
    (206) 747-3411

Distributed in Canada by
    Raincoast Books
    112 East Third Avenue
    Vancouver, British Columbia V5T 1C8
    (604) 874-1111

To that dashing Scot and his
charming Southern Belle,
an old Scottish toast:

*"Here's tae us*
*Wha's like us?*
*No' many*
*And they're a deid."*

# Contents

## 1

## "Challenge, Excitement, Adventure… Jesus, It's Ancient."    

*"When you go to Alaska, it's kind of like going to the far ends of the earth. You pack your damn kit bag and maybe you'll see them later and maybe you won't," says Bill Brown, who with his salt-and-pepper beard looks like one of the original pioneers.*

## 2

## The Only People    

*Sadie Neokok lives on the coast of the frozen Arctic Ocean. Small and engaging with lively brown eyes, she is Inupiat Eskimo. Inupiat means the real people, the only people. "We were so isolated. We always felt we were the only people."*

## 3

## The Scatter Kid, Prince Of The Pike    

*Behind his bar at the Rainbow saloon is a little red book printed in 1946 entitled* Playing the Field: The Autobiography of an All-American Racketeer *by Diamond Spike. Scatter Edwards' name is listed with the worst of them. He was the youngest pimp of them all.*

# Alaska: Place Names In Characters' Stories

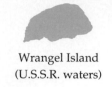

Wrangel Island
(U.S.S.R. waters)

Saint
Lawrence
Island

*BERING*

*SEA*

ALEUTIAN

ISLANDS

Unimak Island
Cape Sarichef
Scotch C

Samalga
Island

Unalaska Island
Dutch Harbor

*ARCTIC*                                    *OCEAN*

Barrow

Wainwright

Pt. Hope

Cape
Prince of
Wales

B R O O K S    R A N G E

Nome

*Yukon River*

Fairbanks

Eagle

*Charley River*

Iditarod

Mt. McKinley

Aniak

*Susitna River*          Willow
                         *Nancy Lake*

Bethel

WRANGELL
MOUNTAINS

Mt. Susitna

Knik

Anchorage

Soldotna

Kasilof            Bird Creek    Girdwood
*Kenai River*
*Kenai Lake*

Seward

Homer

Seldovia

*Resurrection Bay*

*Kachemak Bay*

*Halibut Cove*
*Bear Cove*

*Prince William*
*Sound*

Yakutat

Skagway

*Lituya Bay*

Cape Spencer

*Glacier Bay*

Juneau

*Tracy Arm*

ALASKA

Kodiak

PENINSULA

*GULF OF ALASKA*

Petersburg

Ketchikan

Annette Island

Metlakatla

*(Map illustration by Wanda Seamster)*

# Introduction

Alaska has many different characters. These are only a few.

There are good guys, bad guys, escapists, opportunists, romantics, pioneers, adventurers, hard workers, scoundrels, and dandies.

Alaska is a melting pot. It is no longer a tapestry of Native cultures. English is spoken with every imaginable accent from Tlingit to Italian to southern drawl. There are those whose families have been here for centuries and those who recently pulled up roots to come. They came from the north and the south, from across the ocean and over the pole, from small farms and the world's largest cities.

One thing Alaskans have in common: they either love this place or they hate it—sometimes in the same week. There is nothing lukewarm about living here.

So who are these Alaskans?

Thousands of years ago, crossing from one continent to the next, the ancestors of the people we know as

*Twin Lakes, Alaska Peninsula.*
*(National Park Service)*

*There is a spirit in the north country, powerful and contagious. It seeps into your bones. Some say that after one year in Alaska, a person isn't fit to live on the Outside anymore. They say Alaskans are just a little bit mad. Perhaps. But perhaps, like the gold rush poet Robert Service once wrote, they are touched by the forces of this great, big, broad land and caught by a beauty that is "haunting and haunting."*

Indians, Eskimos, and Aleuts were the first people to set foot in North America. Isolated from the rest of the world by frozen seas and dark, forbidding mountains, they lived in relative harmony with the land and seasons.

Of the more recent arrivals, many came north for adventure or escape. Others came to get rich quick—from gold or oil or the pockets of their neighbors. Still others arrived, looked at this frozen wasteland in horror, and ran fast for the first boat or plane headed south. The arctic cold has a way of chasing people out.

But some stayed. And this is what these stories are about.

There is a spirit in the north country, powerful and contagious. It seeps into your bones. Some say that after one year in Alaska, a person isn't fit to live on the Outside anymore. They say Alaskans are just a little bit mad. Perhaps. But perhaps, like the gold rush poet Robert Service once wrote, they are touched by the forces of this great, big, broad land and caught by a beauty that is "haunting and haunting."

As the old weathered prospector told newcomer Billy Spear one rainy evening as they sat together in a dark bar in Juneau: "You know, if you stay up here long enough, one day you'll be sitting somewhere and you'll look up. And there will be a scene so emotionally moving and so powerful that wherever you go in the world, that scene will always appear to you and draw you back to the north . . ."

*Turquoise Lake region, Lake Clark National Park.* (National Park Service)

# EADQUARTERS

## ONAL PARK

# 1

## "Challenge, Excitement, Adventure...Jesus, It's Ancient."

**W**hen you go to Alaska, it's kind of like going to the far ends of the earth. You pack your damn kit bag and maybe you'll see them later and maybe you won't," says Bill Brown, who with his salt-and-pepper beard looks like one of the original pioneers.

"Alaska has always offered some promise to either get rich quick or to have some room to maneuver—to get away from a society that was getting too crowded else-where. Apart from the indigenous peoples, most of the people who came were a bit on the fringes of more estab-lished populations. Another way of putting it is that I think there are a lot of crazies in Alaska, a hell of a lot of people who don't fit in."

There's a boyishness about Bill. He has an adven-turer in his soul. Eloquent and intense, he speaks about this land and the people who live here through the observant eyes of a historian. But he is not a spectator. He, too, is part of the romance and poetry of Alaska, one of the "crazies"

*Wrangell-St. Elias National Park in Alaska. (National Park Service)*
Inset: *Bill Brown, park historian at Denali National Park. (Nan Elliot)*

*"Hell, all of Alaska is damn near as big as the United States east of the Mississippi and the population is not even as big as one of the neighborhoods in New York City. That's one of the great things about it."*

who has sunk his feet deep into this wilderness soil.

"As far as who Alaskans are, you have to make a division between the recent arrivals and the people who have been here for centuries. The Native people have been here a very long time and some Euro-Americans for a shorter time but still two or three generations. Then there are the recent arrivals—the people who came up for bureaucratic reasons.

"Whether it's New Spain, Russian Alaska, or Alaska today, if you live in an outpost of a larger society, you're going to have a high incidence of government employment. So you have a lot of government people and others who arrived with the great surge of the latest extractive boom, which is, of course, oil and gas. Then you've got the people who just want to be close to the country, who arrive saying, 'I want to build a log cabin. I want to hunt. I want to have a rifle. Or I just want to be in the woods.'

"For the traditional Native people, Alaska is not a raw frontier. It's their home. They're not here for some kind of thrill or to prove something. They're here because they've been here for a thousand years in traceable generations or longer. It's home. It's their backyard. That's a very different attitude than one of coming up here with seven-league boots on for a kind of Walter Mitty release. They have a different view of the land. It's not a place where you fulfill fantasies. It's a place where you live in measured consonance with the way the world is.

"Of course, they're undergoing a lot of changes. There's no monolithic Native presence in Alaska either. They're culturally and philosophically diverse. They have partaken in many, many cultural cups. But basically, the people who have been here for a while do not represent some kind of high-adrenaline, Dionysian approach to Alaska. They're not

*Hikers at Denali National Park.* (John Kauffmann, National Park Service)

*Yentna Glacier, Denali National Park.* (National Park Service)

*Dall sheep at Denali National Park.*
(National Park Service)

out to get it or take it over. They don't look on Alaska as something to whip around to their own preconceived notions. There is still a strong traditional notion of staying within the bounds of the country, living with it, rather than transforming it to something else.

"The old-timers, the Euro-Americans, most of them came for one reason. There were big bucks in some kind of extractive quest, whether it was the Russians hunting for furs or the Americans following gold, timber, fish, or the more recent booms of oil and gas.

"But also, a hell of a lot of people, who are today's older Alaska residents, are people who came up during World War II, not because they made a choice, but because they were driven. Now that's the way migrations occur. You were drafted and sent up to fight in the Aleutians or build the Alaska Highway. Once here, two kinds of things could happen. Either you really got into the country

*Alatna River, Brooks Range.* (National Park Service)

"Alaska has always offered some promise to either get rich quick or to have some room to maneuver. . . . Most of the people who came were a bit on the fringes of more established populations. Another way of putting it is that I think there are a lot of crazies in Alaska, a hell of a lot of people who don't fit in."

and you said, 'Jesus, this is where I want to live' or you said 'Let me out of this goddamn place.'

"So you have a high selection of people, if you're speaking in biological terms, who are more individualistic. Some very interesting people. Even though there's only half a million people here, not too long ago before the oil boom, there were 200,000 people spread around the state. Even at that, hell, all of Alaska is damn near as big as the United States east of the Mississippi and the population is not even as big as one of the neighborhoods in New York City. That's one of the great things about it.

"There is a brash population in Alaska of those who want to go out and whip it and get it. Very few of the older Alaskans, those who have been here for 40 or 50 years, are part of that attitude.

"I can think of a number of very gentle people I know who simply want to fit into the landscape and have a very good, solid, traditional life. Some of the people I know in Eagle on the Yukon River are like this. They see Eagle as a small community that preserves some of the cultural traditions of the Euro-American world. It's a small village with people being accountable to one another, lending each other a helping hand. That's another element that's part of the romance of Alaska too—small groups of people who can be supportive and traditionally sound. We don't all have to be crazies.

"When I say crazy, I don't mean someone who is totally nuts. What I mean is people who have a very short fuse. What they're trying to do is get space. I think they need social and personal space. Alaska provides that. At least the idea provides it. Even if they never get out of Anchorage, they say, 'Jesus, I'd never live down in the Lower 48—all those regulations, all those people. Sure am glad I live in Alaska.'

"The frontier spirit may be a romantic notion. Then again, it may be a hard-nose, driving necessity to go out and challenge oneself, the world, whatever. Challenge, excitement, adventure—Jesus, it's ancient."

Bill Brown was born in the Pacific Northwest in 1930. As a child, he roamed the wide open spaces of the lake country. As an adolescent, he went to live with his grandfather in a picturesque orange grove nestled against the desert mountains of southern California.

"I experienced the western states in those Elysian, balmy days when they were romantically beautiful places," he remembers. Joining the National Park Service as a historian in 1957, he has worked in New England, the deep South, and the Southwest. He loved the Southwest in particular. It was a place a generation behind in development and still isolated. But the forces of progress were relentless. He watched with dismay as the power plants moved in, coal mines expanded, and resources were ripped from the earth until it turned into "a utility backyard for the rest of the world."

"After a number of years in the Southwest watching it decline, I guess I got itchy again. You see, my ancestors were people that came across on the Oregon Trail. I have it in my blood.

"I came to Alaska in 1975 to work on Yukon-Charley (one of the park proposals for inclusion in the National Park Service system). That got me out in the country. I was very fortunate in the sense that I had an arena with an institutional base that allowed me immediately to get away from the city and fulfill some of those needs that I've been talking about. I didn't just fly up there, keep the propeller running, and run back to the plane. I spent all kinds of time out there, went out into the country, hiking in the summer and going by dog team in the winter. I got to know people."

*The Arrigetch Peaks, Brooks Range.*
*(John Kauffmann, National Park Service)*

*The Brooks Range, Gates of the Arctic National Park.* (National Park Service)

In 1980, by an act of the United States Congress, Bill Brown's beloved country where the swift, clear waters of the Charley River merge with the mighty Yukon became part of the National Park system. It was one of 15 wild, scenic, and historic areas of Alaska to be included in the national parks. The inclusion of Alaska's lands doubled the size of the national park system in the United States.

In 1982, Bill wrote a lovely, lyrical book about the new park lands in Alaska and called it *This Last Treasure*. In his foreword, he wrote:
"*. . . Alaska is a gathering of mythic landscapes, asked to meet here by God or Nature . . . Scale and diversity foil all who try to simplify Alaska. Its immense and ceaseless grandeur numbs the mind, glazes the eye, and plagues the writer who would describe it. The intellect cannot close the* *suitcase on this sub-continent. Always a spare peninsula or archipelago or coastal plain dangles out . . .*"

Now in his late 50s, Bill has just finished writing a book about the "ultimate wilderness," that last magnificent range of mountains in arctic Alaska before the land stretches flat and treeless to the Arctic Ocean—the Brooks Range. Every morning, he runs five miles to stockpile energy as a match for the exuberance of his

*"When you go to Alaska, it's kind of like going to the far ends of the earth. You pack your damn kit bag and maybe you'll see them later and maybe you won't."*

two young sons. He splits his time these days between the arctic wilderness, the wilds of Denali National Park, and the little town of Gustavus on the outskirts of Glacier Bay in southeast Alaska where his wife, Carolyn, once a ranger in Glacier Bay National Park, built a summer cabin.

"What's happened to me is exactly what I've been talking about," Bill reflects. "I want to become rooted in this place. That's why a lot of people who came during the gold rush ended up living in a place like Eagle or Fairbanks, cutting wood, running dogs, gardening, or trapping. They didn't make a dime on gold. But they found a way to stay and on their own terms.

"This is my home forever. I'm not leaving."

*Bill Brown charts his course on Sheep Ridge overlooking the Charley River in interior Alaska.* (National Park Service)

# 2

# The Only People

**F**or two months, the people live in darkness.

The sun sets on the Arctic coast every year in the middle of November. It does not rise again until the end of January. Bitter cold winds blow and temperatures drop well below zero.

"We are Inupiat. We are the people. We are the real people, the only people. That is what Inupiat means. We were so isolated that we always felt we were the only people. We have always depended on the land and animals," says Sadie Neokok, a tiny Eskimo lady in her 70s with gray hair and lively brown eyes. She is sawing up a side of caribou she has just hauled back from her underground frozen cellar out at fish camp, 23 miles across the tundra and lakes of the Arctic coast. There are no roads there. The journey takes two hours over the tundra by skidoo.

Barrow, where Sadie lives, lies 330 miles north of the Arctic Circle at the edge of the frozen Arctic Ocean.

Sadie's little green house stands on the gravel beach.

*Whaling in the Arctic Ocean around the turn of the century. (Lomen Brothers Collection, University of Alaska Fairbanks)*

*"We are Inupiat. We are the people. We are the real people, the only people. That is what Inupiat means. We were so isolated that we always felt we were the only people."*

Only in the middle of summer with midnight sun and 24 hours of daylight is there open water by the coast. But this July, the winds have blown the ice pack up on shore. It is a surrealistic sight. Huge chunks of ice are stacked up on the rocks and massive towers of sculpted ice float in the water as far north to the horizon as one can see. Only a few feet from the beach, the dust from the dirt roads of Barrow clogs the air and the golden-green grasses of the tundra wave softly in the breezes. When the breezes are still, the mosquitoes are thick and blood-thirsty.

Sadie slaps on mosquito repellent to ward off the hordes. In the old days, she would build a green willow fire and stand in the smoke to cut her fish or skin caribou. Despite the vicious insects, summer is her favorite time.

"Each animal has its season. But in the summer you can hunt everything. Right now, the caribou are nice and fat," says Sadie with a merry twinkle in her eyes.

She is the daughter of the famous whaler and trader Charles Brower, whose story *Fifty Years Below Zero: A Lifetime of Adventure in the Far North* is a classic in Alaska literature. Brower started a whaling and trading station on the Arctic coast in the late 1800s. It was 12 miles from the village where the "Point Barrow People" lived. But they built a school there. Today, the old whaling station is the site of the town of Barrow. With the discovery of oil on the North Slope of Alaska, the population has swelled to 5,000.

One of the original residents, this tiny woman is also one of the most respected. She never had any legal training. But she was appointed by the governor of Alaska as the first woman judge on the Arctic coast and served for 20 years.

The kitchen table was her judge's bench. She worked far longer than she ever intended. The people would not let her retire.

"When a man is found guilty, I don't sentence him right away," she says. "I look into his family. I go and talk with his wife. I see

*Sadie Neokok and one of her grandsons stand outside her home on the frozen beach of the Arctic Ocean.* (Nan Elliot)

how the children would live if they would be deprived of a father or a mother. Who would take care of the family? And then I act accordingly. People trust me to give a fair sentence."

Sadie and her husband, Nate, are known to everyone on the North Slope. As a whaling captain, Nate holds the most prestigious rank in Eskimo society. Until this century, the Eskimos of the Arctic were a nomadic people, living entirely from the land and sea, tailoring their culture to one of the most extreme climates on earth. To be a great hunter was the noblest of all distinctions. Still today, a good whaling captain is highly respected.

The big whale hunting season is in the spring. This year, the people of Barrow caught eight whales. There was much celebration.

"The whale is a spiritual animal, a very clean animal to us, a sacred animal," says Sadie.

"Everything has to be clean before you start hunting—the clothing, the hunting gear, the place where you store the meat. This is a tradition with us, handed down from our ancestors. You don't chase the whale. It comes to you. If the water is calm and your boat is ready, then you can paddle out and greet it.

"The man who puts the first harpoon into it, he's the owner of

"The whale is a spiritual animal . . . a sacred animal. You don't chase the whale. It comes to you. If the water is calm and your boat is ready, then you can paddle out and greet it."

During spring season in the Arctic Ocean, Eskimo whalers from Barrow divide and share the meat, muktuk, and blubber of their catch with all the people in town. The muktuk is the skin of the whale, about two inches thick. "Ohhh, it's delicious when the muktuk is fresh and right off the whale," says Sadie. "It's like having fresh clams or oysters." (Bill Hess)

*At festival time, the singing is loud, the drumming is long, and the feasting brings great sighs of happiness. The lean, dark winter is over.*

*Blanket toss, Whale-Catch Festival, Barrow. (Bill Hess)*

the whale. But everybody gets a share of the meat. Each crew member—there are 13 or more—will get a big share. The whaling captain is the prosperous one. He gets the biggest portion. But he also must feed the whole town the same day he brings in the whale. At the Whale-Catch Festival (mid- to late June), he must serve the people the choicest part of the tail flukes and meat.

"For the festival, we boil the heart, the intestines, the kidney, the meat, and the muktuk. The rest of it is just raw, in chunks. Everybody goes out with their pots and pans and we serve them from morning to night.

"Ohhh, it's delicious when the muktuk is fresh and right off the whale. You boil it. It's like having fresh clams or oysters." Sadie rolls her eyes and pats her stomach. The muktuk is the skin of the whale about two inches thick. Underneath that is about a foot of blubber, she explains. "At Thanksgiving potluck and Christmas, we bring the whale out again. But we don't boil it then. It would taste like an old boot sole," she grimaces. "We serve it frozen."

After the meat is taken, the people sink the bones of the whale to let its spirit go free.

"When our people hunt and kill an animal, our custom is to pour fresh water into its mouth.

*An Eskimo hunter on the ice floes of the Arctic Ocean, circa 1920.*
*(Lomen Brothers Collection, University of Alaska Fairbanks)*

This brings the animal spirit back. Every year, the whale returns to us," says Sadie.

Eskimo people all along the Arctic coast have a special reverence for the whale. An old Eskimo lady visiting from Point Hope, a village to the west of Barrow, says the people of her village never eat the meat of the whale's head. "We believe that you may take from the sea, but you must also give something back. We sink the head back into the ocean. Terrible things happened once when two whalers took parts of a whale head for themselves. They soon died frightful deaths."

For centuries, Alaska Native peoples have tapped the bounty of the land and ocean, savoring foods enjoyed few other places in the world. Depending on the season, a sampling from the festival table might include fermented whale blubber, rotten fish heads, raw walrus flipper, frozen bone marrow, moose head soup, or caribou meat dipped in rancid seal oil. While such an offering might send some stomachs spinning, it is the very heart and soul of an old traditional way of life.

"During the long winter, we get so hungry for fresh whale meat again," says Sadie with a long sigh. "You wouldn't believe how tender it is. We let it ferment about two weeks in its own blood. You must stir it every day until the blood thickens. You mustn't let it get bloated. When it ages, that raw meat has the taste of sweet berries. At whale festival time, we serve big buckets of it."

*"My mom was the most wonderful woman,"* remembers Sadie. *"The people here were so poor. And she took care of them. My dad had the trading post. My mother would walk into the store and go through the shelves with a big bag. 'Who's hungry today, Bones?' He'd talk to her in Eskimo. She was so skinny when they first met. She never had an English name. So he called her 'Bones.' The name stuck."*

The whaling festival is several days of feasting, dancing, and singing. It is a nostalgic time for those who cannot make it home. In the museum in Anchorage stands a powerful Eskimo drummer, carved from alabaster. There is an intensity of expression on his face. He is singing, harmonizing with the large, flat drum in his hands. Carved one wistful spring when its creator, sculptor Larry Ahvakana, a native son of Barrow, could not make it home for whaling festival, the drummer instead became his celebration.

The drum is made from the skin of a young caribou. It is sanded down very thin for the right tone and sound and then stretched over a circular frame. The drummer holds it vertically and then beats it with a stick from behind.

Eskimos say if the drum is right, you feel like you want to sing loudly.

At festival time, the singing is loud, the drumming is long, and the feasting brings great sighs of happiness. The lean, dark winter is over.

Sadie Neokok has seen many lean winters on this icy, wind-swept coast. She was born in 1916, one of 14 children. Her mother was Inupiat. Her father, Charles Brower, the son of Dutch immigrants, was born in New York while his father was off fighting in the Civil War. By the time he was 21 years old, he'd been at sea for seven years.

As he later wrote, he never dreamed that the fashioning of ladies' corsets would shape his destiny. Without corsets, there was little demand for whalebone or the great whaling fleets that pursued the whales into the Arctic. Despite the dangers, hardship, and often violent death, there were fabulous profits to be made from the flexible whalebone or baleen which hung from the jaws of the great polar whale.

Brower first came to Alaska on a coal mining expedition for Pacific Steam Whaling Company in 1877. He was to explore for coal and trade it to the Eskimos for furs, whalebone, and ivory. He lived in Alaska the rest of his life.

In 1902, Brower's first wife, an Eskimo from Point Hope, died in the epidemic of black measles, says Sadie. Her own mother's first husband and their young children also died in the epidemic. So her mother was chosen to take care of the four children her dad already had. One thing led to another. They got interested in each other and got married in 1903.

"My mom was the most wonderful woman," remembers Sadie. "The people here were so poor. And she took care of them. My dad had the trading post. My mother would walk into the store and go through the shelves with a big bag. 'Who's hungry today, Bones?' He'd talk to her in Eskimo. She was so skinny when they first met. She never had an English name. So he called her 'Bones.' The name stuck. Her Eskimo name was Ahseagatuk. It means 'sweet berry.'

"As a little girl, I used to go hunting with my mom. She was quite a hunter. I helped her with fishing, collecting driftwood, hauling wood with her dogteam, feeding the dogs. That was a big chore. I cooked them a mash of seal meat and walrus meat. We hunted caribou by dog team. That took us about five days. The dogs could only travel about 30 miles a day. You had to rest them. My dad loved to hunt, but he had the

Walrus. (National Park Service)

whaling station and trading post, so my mom was the big hunter for the family.

"My first successful hunt, I killed a seal. I was 11. I was walking out on the ice to where the men were whaling. A seal lay sunning himself on the ice next to his blow hole. I began to crawl so he wouldn't see me. I shot him. But he was only injured. Before he could go back down his blow hole, I ran and grabbed his flippers and pulled him back across the ice. In those days, seal blubber was used for heating homes."

There are no trees in the high Arctic. People heated their homes from driftwood and sod. Whole families lived in tiny one-room

*Depending on the season and region of Alaska, a sampling from the festival table might include fermented whale blubber, rotten fish heads, raw walrus flipper, frozen bone marrow, moose head soup, or caribou meat dipped in rancid seal oil.*

*Dancing the Walrus Dance.* (*Lulu Fairbanks Collection, University of Alaska Fairbanks*)

houses. The tuberculosis epidemic in the earlier part of this century swept through those tiny houses, killing whole families at one time.

"It was a heartbreak situation," remembers Sadie.

"When people came to the village, they lived in these cramped houses. No one knew about sanitation. There was hardly enough fuel to keep clean and wash clothes. When they were nomadic, the people never got sick. They were able to keep clean. They killed more animals. That meant a fresh suit of clothes more often and more fresh food. They weren't cooped up in those little sod houses. They built snow houses and lived in skin tents. That's how we live today when we go hunting. You can make a new snow house every week or two. And just a little lamp keeps a snow house warm."

One year, Sadie's father took her Outside on one of the big sailing ships that brought in supplies. She went to high school in San Francisco and qualified for entrance to Stanford University. But she was so homesick that she "soft-talked" her uncle into paying her way home to Barrow.

When Sadie married Nate, he already had the reputation of being a good hunter. "He'd hardly been to school. His education was survival—hunting and trapping.

But he knew more than I did with all my education." Sadie and Nate had 12 children, three girls and nine boys. Today, they have lots of grandchildren who dash in and out of the little house. Over the years, they've taken in a large share of abandoned and neglected children, too.

Their home has been an oasis of warmth for many on the Arctic coast—including famous adventurers.

One day, Sadie got a call from her son. It was April. He and his brothers were cleaning out the cellar. It had seal meat and whale meat. "This is our custom in whaling season. You clean out everything, because the whale is a sacred animal up here among the Eskimo people. My son said, 'We have a man here who would like to have some of the seal meat. He said he traveled all the way from Greenland.'

"I said, 'Feed him. He's a traveler.'

"When I got home, there was this little Japanese man—the most pleasant man you'd ever want to meet—down on he floor with a map telling Nate where he'd been. He'd gotten so used to raw seal meat, he wanted some for him and his dogs."

The man was Naomi Uemura, a national hero and legend in Japan, adored by millions of his countrymen and admired around the world. He was the first Japanese climber to reach the summit of Mt. Everest and the first climber to scale Mt. McKinley solo in the spring of 1969. Now he was mushing his dogs alone across the Arctic from Greenland to the Bering Sea coast.

"He spoke very little English, but he talked a lot," smiles Sadie, remembering. "Then he looked up and saw my telephone.

"'Does your telephone reach Tokyo?' he asked. He was on the telephone—bowing and talking and bowing and talking—and saying, 'Ah so!' We didn't understand what he was saying, but we laugh even today to think of it. He wrote to us all the time—many, many letters. We were very sad when we heard on the radio he died on Mt. McKinley."

In 1983, Uemura (on his second trip to the mountain) was the first climber to make it to the summit of McKinley alone in the middle of winter. On his descent, he vanished.

"Is he really dead? I always wonder," says Sadie with a sadness in her eyes. "Up here, when a loved one goes out on the ice and disappears, you wait and wait and wait, always expecting him to show up any time.

"Every year in whaling season a hunter is sure to get lost when

*As a whaling captain, Nate holds the most prestigious rank in Eskimo society. When Sadie married Nate, she says "He'd hardly been to school. His education was survival—hunting and trapping. But he knew more than I did with all my education."*

Above: *Sadie Neokok receives her honorary degree of Doctor of Laws at the University of Alaska Fairbanks in 1987.*
Inset: *Sadie Neokok and her husband Nate, a distinguished whaling captain from Barrow.* (Bill Hess)

the ice on the ocean starts breaking up. Today, we have radios and airplanes to search for them. But in the old days, men went out only with their dog teams. If someone got lost, we waited and waited. If we saw a stray dog wander into town, then we had hopes that somewhere he made it to shore, like the dog, and we would see him again."

# 3

# The Scatter Kid, Prince Of The Pike

Scatter Edwards is a bad guy with a good heart. He's always been on the wrong side of the law.

Behind his bar at the Rainbow Lounge is a little red book, printed in 1946, entitled *Playing the Field: The Autobiography of an All-American Racketeer* by Diamond Spike. Scatter's name is listed with the worst of them. There's no-body in there but pimps, whores, thieves, gamblers, outlaws, rustlers, liars, scoundrels, cheats, and high rollers. Right there, in story and verse, is the tale of "The Scatter Kid: Prince of the Pike," the youngest pimp of them all.

In those rabble-rousing days when Anchorage was a young frontier town, Scatter ran a whorehouse and a string of saloons and ended up in jail for pumping a fellow full of bullets one night.

He's 69 today and a little more mellow. He spent his time in the pokey and gave up the whorehouse since the girls told him they could do better on their own. He just pours booze in one bar now. That is, when he's sober.

He fishes, hunts, swills whiskey, and still chases the girls—he loves them, every one. Along with serving liquor, he's a one-man floor show—comedian, jokester, and storyteller. With a beer in each hand, he's surprisingly lucid for a fellow who's been on a five-day bender.

Still saucy, but a little bleary-eyed from the gallons of beer racing through his veins, he welcomes a young lady into the bar.

"Well, how are you? OK? You still got your clothes on. You look all right. Ain't nobody undressed you yet." He grins.

"You know, if I were 20 years younger, honey," he rolls out the words in a slow amused drawl, "I'd make you a career girl."

"And it wouldn't be writing stories, neither," giggles one whiskey-throated old woman with rouged-up cheeks swinging her legs over a bar stool.

Born and raised in a bar in Louisiana (his father died at the age of 84 and they buried him at the back door of the saloon), Scatter hopped a steamship to Alaska in 1940, just one jump ahead of the law. He was supposed to go into the service. He was 21. But he would have none of it. He says, "There wasn't a war on then. Why the hell should I go into the Army? I just kept moving until they caught up with me

in '41. Took 'em eleven months. Two FBI guys had me and I knew I'd better enlist."

Scatter became a gunner in the U.S. Army Air Corps. Flying out of Africa and Italy during World War II, he completed 50 combat missions and earned a lifelong nickname. He shot a scatter gun from underneath the belly of a B-17 bomber, known as a "Flying Fortress." He says he's one of the few men ever to survive 50 missions.

"You know what the lifetime of a gunner was overseas in combat? Five minutes," he says. "If a son-of-a-bitch ain't scared, he ain't been there. Do you think I worry about anything now? Nothing. I've been there and back."

Story has it that Scatter was drinking in a bar down the road one day and a fellow ran in and yelled, "Scatter, Scatter, the Rainbow is burning."

And Scatter said, "Don't bother me, I'm drinking."

The original Rainbow saloon burnt to the ground.

Scatter's response is, "You been close to death that many times and you gonna worry about some saloon burning?"

After the war, he returned to Alaska. "I wanted to come back here. But I can't tell you why. I don't know why. I like the girls.

*"You know what the lifetime of a gunner was overseas in combat? Five minutes. If a son-of-a-bitch ain't scared, he ain't been there. Do you think I worry about anything now? Nothing. I've been there and back."*

Above: *Scatter's plane: The "Flying Fortress," a B-17 bomber.*
Below: *Scatter, right, a gunner in the U.S. Army Air Corps, flew 50 successful combat missions in World War II and was a decorated hero.*
(Scatter Edwards collection)

I like all of them. I've been married to six of them and I've never had but two good ones—the one that's left and the one I was getting." He chuckles and tips his can of beer. It's obviously a line he's been fond of for years.

Someone at the pool table calls out, "Hey, Scatter, were you really a pimp?"

Scatter pauses, then answers in a slow, warm, southern drawl. "I went to jail for shooting a fellow and running a whorehouse. I guess I was pimping. I knocked a fisherman in the head and burned his plant down 'cause he tore my whorehouse up. I guess I was pimping. Ask Judge Moody. He was the one who sent me to jail. He was the district attorney then. He's a judge now. And we're still buddies. We drink together every time I see him. Only he got his stomach all taken out and he can't drink no more. So I got one up on him. He's a wonderful man. Lot of people don't like him. But he's honest. Hell, if you could have bought him, I wouldn't have gone to jail.

"It cost me $40,000 for a lawyer to defend me—Stanley McCutcheon—and I still went to jail. McCutcheon's dead and gone now. But during my trial, he used to change his shirt, change his socks, and change his clothes at every recess. He'd get up there and cry and beg and plead. He didn't give a goddamn about me. He was just up there floor-showing.

"This fellow thought he was Clarence Darrow. He had them women all wrapped up. I never will forget his closing argument.

"He said, 'If you can send this young man to the penitentiary—this man who flew 50 missions in the Air Force—then what are we fighting for? What is our country for? If you send him to jail, we ain't got no democracy.' He's crying. Tears are running down his cheeks. He's down on his knees, praying and begging." Scatter grins at the memory. "But he don't give a goddamn if I go to jail. He's already got my money."

Scatter was sent to prison to serve three concurrent two-year sentences and was turned loose on parole eight months later. He swears he didn't shoot the fellow out of meanness. The man smashed a stool through Scatter's back bar mirror down in the Frontier Saloon. The law of the Wild West prevailed. Scatter shot him. "I didn't do nobody wrong that didn't try to do me wrong first. Life's really simple. Right is right and wrong is wrong. You treat everybody the way you want to be treated. That's part of the Ten Commandments. That's all

*The pope and the president were arriving for a historic meeting in Fairbanks, Alaska. Scatter was also returning home that Wednesday from vacation. A neighbor put this sign up on the highway outside the Rainbow Lounge. Scatter pinned up a photo of the sign next to his sacred fish thermometer.*
(Ted Bell)

the religion I got. My daddy taught me that."

A murmur of agreement ripples through the clientele at the bar. Over in the corner burbles a big pot of Scatter's famous Louisiana beans. They're free—always have been. Scatter cooks them up every morning, just like his daddy used to do back home.

A sandy-haired gent with the slowest drawl this side of Georgia confides, "I have come in here many times, hungry as hell, and eaten a mess of these Louisiana

beans. Scatter's fed a powerful lot of hungry men in his day and never charged a dime."

But back to the infamous red book and the even more infamous author who went to school to become a priest and turned out a pimp. Diamond Spike was quite a bit older than The Scatter Kid. But they'd been through a few tense poker games before the classy gambler wrote his memoirs.

"Diamond always walked out of the bedroom dressed like a

*Behind his bar at the Rainbow Lounge is a little red book, printed in 1946, entitled* Playing the Field: The Autobiography of an All-American Racketeer *by Diamond Spike. Scatter's name is listed with the worst of them. There's nobody in there but pimps, whores, thieves, gamblers, outlaws, rustlers, liars, scoundrels, cheats, and high rollers.*

millionaire. He'd be clean shaven with a diamond stickpin in his tie and spats on his shoes. He was a real gentleman," remembers Scatter with fondness.

"One day, Diamond Spike asked me if I thought we could get in on that twenty-one game up on the railroad. I said sure. But he ain't got no money. And I ain't got no money.

"'Well,' he said, 'go down and get some of those dollar wrappers. Then go to the hardware store and buy some washers.' He rolled them up and put them on that twenty-one table. All rolled up, they looked real impressive, but there wasn't any money in them.

"I said, 'What if we lose?'

"He looked at me and said, 'I'm dealing. There ain't gonna be no losing.'"

At the memory of it all Scatter roars with laughter. "That son-of-a-bitch was somethin' else. He sure could deal a deck of cards. There ain't never been an honest deck of cards invented."

Dice was Scatter's game.

He claims he brought real gambling to this country—"real, honest gambling where you win all the time." He'd strap a magnet to his leg and shoot with loaded dice. But, just in case, he kept a loaded pistol in his pocket. Nobody was going to be asking any questions if they ever found out he was cheating.

Over in the corner of the Rainbow Lounge, someone slips a quarter in the jukebox and punches Scatter's favorite country western tune: "I Got Swinging Doors, a Jukebox, and a Bar Stool."

Yep. He's pretty content here at the Rainbow.

Like his daddy, he just might camp here in this little dilapidated bar until that last swallow of beer, dishing out booze and free beans, telling ribald stories, and making people laugh. But he doesn't want to be buried out the back door.

"Just throw me off the Homer spit. Those crabs and shrimp will get rid of me in a few minutes. I've been eating 'em all my life. I want to give 'em a chance to get even."

# 4

# Pulitzer Prize-Winner Jim Babb: "We're All Mad."

I n my generation, in the 1960s, a lot of us just quietly got out of the country. You went as far as you could go with hot and cold running water . . . maybe . . . and still stay in the United States of America. Somewhere where you didn't have to put up with all those things that went along with the Vietnam War . . . the surveillance, the wire-tapping, the polarization."

Years ago, as editor of the statewide Alaska Native newspaper, *The Tundra Times*, village people called Jim Babb "the red-haired Eskimo." He is a former Pulitzer Prize-winning reporter, editor, professor, and foundation administrator, and today describes himself with his sharp and cynical sense of humor as "a gutter lawyer . . . as ever, trying to do good by doing well and managing thusly about 51 percent." As a lawyer committed to social justice, he may, as he says, "make changes and force consequences," but he will never be rich. Yet, as one of his colleagues who shared in the Pulitzer Prize wrote him

*Newspaperman Jim Babb: "Like everyone else, I only came for two years, right? Then I was going out to a bigger newspaper. But you know my theory on carbon monoxide poisoning? The cliche is that once you've spent two winters in Fairbanks you may leave, but you always come back." (Rob Stapleton)*

recently: " . . . we're all rich where it matters most, if we want to be, and that's enough for guys like us."

Now on the eve of his 53rd birthday, Jim came to Alaska when he was 29 years old.

"Many of us came here because we believed personally, professionally, and institutionally that we could avoid making the mistakes that had screwed up society so badly down there. Here we could do it right. So that takes on the complexion of an opportunity with a fairly noble motive. We were going to a new place and do something different and get away from a whole specter of things—pollution, race riots, the Vietnam War, and government interference. A number of people came up like I did, but it was an unconscious motivation. I don't think we ever articulated it.

"During those years, being in Alaska was like sitting on a mountain top. You had a sense of perspective. Whether you did or not is another question. But there was time for reflection."

Jim Babb left an executive position with a small research firm in Washington, D.C., and moved his family to Fairbanks, Alaska, in 1966. He had seen an advertisement for a general assignment reporter for the *Fairbanks Daily News Miner*. As a young boy, he

had spent three years of his childhood on Kodiak Island in Alaska. His father was a captain in the U.S. Navy. Jim remembered it as one of the most beautiful places he'd ever seen. That summer of 1966 Washington, D.C., was hot, muggy, and miserable. Within 10 days after he had sent a resume, Jim was hired, had his suitcases packed, and was on his way north.

"Like everyone else, I only came for two years, right? A year or two and then I was going out to a bigger newspaper. But you know my theory on carbon monoxide poisoning? The cliche is that once you've spent two winters in Fairbanks you may leave, but you always come back. That's true for a lot of us. I tested it by going Outside for three years of law school. I went berserk. I just wasn't fit to live out there anymore. I don't know why.

"My theory is that during the winter you're sitting in these locked-up houses where the temperature differential is 130 degrees. When you open the door and walk out of your house, you're walking from 70 degrees above zero to 60 degrees below. That's 130 goddamn degrees. January in Fairbanks. It's a major problem and documented. In those houses and department stores, the carbon monoxide and carbon dioxide

*"Many of us came here because we believed personally, professionally, and institutionally that we could avoid making the mistakes that had screwed up society so badly down there. Here we could do it right. So that takes on the complexion of an opportunity with a fairly noble motive."*

Above: *Newsroom of the* Anchorage Daily News *in 1976 as publisher Kay Fanning opens the Pulitzer Prize award. Jim Babb is standing in the back on the far left.* Inset: *Publisher Kay Fanning with the* Daily News *team of Pulitzer Prize-winning reporters: (left to right) Jim Babb, Bob Porterfield, and Howard Weaver.* (Anchorage Daily News)

levels go much higher than other places where you can open the windows and have fresh air circulating.

"Carbon monoxide is a lethal poison that destroys brain cells. That's my theory. We're all mad."

Jim's face crinkles with humor. He chuckles delightedly.

In 1972, after six years in Fairbanks, Jim Babb went Outside to law school—"not to be a lawyer, but to be a better journalist."

No matter what titles he has held, Jim will always be a newspaperman at heart. He has a visage straight out of Central Casting in Hollywood. He is the classic

newsroom editor, crusty and seasoned, his face lined with the pressures of years on deadline. He can roar with indignation, pound the desk, whoop with laughter, or play the role of the tough guy if need be.

When one of his law professors asked him what he was going

to do upon return, he said, "I'm going back to Alaska and win a goddamn Pulitzer Prize." And he did. He went to work for the *Anchorage Daily News* and with two other reporters—Howard Weaver, now managing editor of the *News*, which won a second Pulitzer in 1989, and Bob Porterfield, who later went on to win two more Pulitzer Prizes with east coast newspapers—wrote a series of investigative stories on the growth of the Teamsters Union's empire in Alaska during construction of the Trans-Alaska Pipeline. They won journalism's most coveted award. That was 1976.

"Five minutes after news of the award came over the wires, Bonnie walked into the office. I said, 'Bonnie, we won the Pulitzer Prize' and she said, 'Jim, we're going to have another baby in December.' So there, at the high point of my career, I knew I couldn't afford to keep on with the newspaper. There's not enough money in it. Not in Alaska. Not with a wife and three children."

Although Jim desperately tries to maintain his image as the authoritarian father, his three funny, red-headed children with their own brand of unconventional humor have blown his cover. If the truth be known, he's a doting father and a soft touch. But not in the courtroom. As a

The red-haired Babb Family in 1989: Caitlin, Jim, Mike, and Bonnie. At school: Brendan. (Nan Elliot)

lawyer, he can write and talk circles around most using the King's English with distinctive flair and ruthless precision. Yet, he is often wistful for his newspaper days. He says if he had a dime for every time he wished he were back at the paper, his eldest son Brendan would be going to Harvard University and his 18-year-old daughter Caitlin (he smiles in mock malice) would be sent to "an exorbitantly expensive convent in San Francisco with high walls with broken glass embedded in the tops."

At the height of his Pulitzer Prize glory, Jim Babb could have written his ticket for considerably more money at any newspaper around the country. Yet he chose to stay in Alaska. Why?

"I can't explain except by analogy. In other places, too often a lawyer is a lawyer is a lawyer. An accountant is an accountant is an accountant. Because of the smallness of the population, because of the issues, because of the problems in Alaska, what you have is a horizontal society rather than a vertical one. So you can go to a party and find the chief justice of the Alaska Supreme Court in a cogent argu-

*When Jim Babb first hung out his shingle, he tacked this photo to his office door with the inscription: "Not just another lawyer."* (Rob Stapleton)

ment about some piece of literature with the local plumber and the plumber may be winning and, in some instances, is just as well informed as the Harvard-educated, well-credentialed person.

"Part of the reason I stay is that I love the winter. The nice thing about winter is that it chases out a lot of people. There's a lot of indigenous greed here in Anchorage. Anchorage has as much to do with Alaska as Toledo, Ohio. But the jobs are here. Most of my friends in this city are ex-Fairbanksians. If they could earn a living in Fairbanks, they'd live there. It's a surprisingly cosmopolitan city.

"There's a tremendous tolerance in Fairbanks for ideas and behavior, a tolerance for human frailties. Some day your car may break down when it's 40 below and that guy driving by may save your damn life. It's that simple. So you don't gratuitously do him in. How that translates, that tolerance, is that there is a degree of respect for the individual human being. Hell, there's lots of room for that.

"The other thing is that none of us are anonymous. You have the sense of being able to control or influence your own life. It may be spurious, but you do have that sense of being a person who counts, who's going to make a difference. In modern-day America, that's an extremely valuable feeling, even if it's wrong, because you do try to make a difference. And you just might.

"It may be a myth, but I really believe that when I go back east to the oak room of some major hotel in New York, for instance, and go to the bar, if there's an Alaskan there, I'll know it. I don't know what it is that we do. I think there's an openness and a penchant to laugh. Four or five times I've been sitting at a bar Outside and all of a sudden a drink will arrive in front of me. The bartender will point to some stranger down the bar and the guy'll lift his glass and grin. It'll be another Alaskan."

Is there anything that would drive Jim Babb out of Alaska?

"Yes," he says with a clipped laugh. "Fantastic wealth."

Where would he go?

"Everywhere . . .

" . . . but then I'd come back."

# 5

# "...All You Have To Do Is Get Up In Front Of Two Billion Men And Dance."

I was terrorized.

"As soon as I went into the bar, I told the bartender, 'I need a shot of whiskey right now and in about 10 minutes I need another one.' He thought it was hilarious. But he also thought I was a big-time dancer from San Francisco.

"He didn't know I was this little Quaker bride about to toss off her pantaloons! Oh, god!" Joan Daniels laughs uproariously.

In 1966, Joan came to Alaska as a go-go dancer. She was 25 years old, a mother with two little girls, Scarlet, 8, and Sara, 7. She wore her long brown hair pulled back in a bun, ran a rooming house for university students in Seattle, and baked a zillion batches of sour cream cookies a day. She loved to sew, garden, cook exotic meals, and take care of everybody's little troubles. She was known fondly as "Mother Joan." Barely older than her boarders, she'd still been running a

*Joan Daniels: "I'm a wild thing, that's for sure. It can't be helped."*
*(Nan Elliot)*

household for many years. She'd gotten pregnant at 16.

"In those days, they wouldn't let you put a toenail in school if you were pregnant. Are you kidding? If you were pregnant, you knew something that no one else should know," says Joan, a handsome woman in her late 40s with a spitfire wit and infectious humor. So, at age 16, she dropped out of school and married her high school sweetheart, the captain of the football team.

All during her childhood, Joan had dreamed of being a pioneer woman. She was born on a farm in Ohio. The woods were full of scary snakes, but also all the beautiful things she loved—bittersweet, hickory nuts, blackberries, flowers, squirrels, deer, and yellow warblers. It was paradise. Then when she was nine, her mother moved the family west to rattlesnake and sagebrush country. It was a shattering experience. Joan had to give up her little empire of woods and fields for the barren dry desert country of eastern Washington. Every night for a year, she hid beneath the covers of her bed and died a thousand deaths.

It was then she promised herself that she was going to find another paradise in the woods. Nothing less than the hydrogen bomb would shake her loose again.

"I *lived* in the pioneer section of the library. I was Narcissa Whitman. I was everybody who ever went on the Oregon Trail," remembers Joan. "The only frontier trail left was to Alaska.

"But my husband was as much of a pioneer as a ladybug. He had no intention of going out and brutalizing his body. He preferred the intellectual life. His parents even offered to grubstake us in Alaska, but he would have nothing to do with it. So that was a nightmare for me. Excess baggage: 6'4" and 200 pounds. I thought, 'I can't carry him. What am I going to do?'"

She struck out on her own. She opened the boarding house and stashed her pennies away for college tuition in Alaska. But she was about to embark on a higher education, the likes of which she had never dreamed.

"A girl I knew answered an ad. She went to Alaska as a dancer in one of the bars. She came back and said, 'Joan, *this is it!* You've got to do it.'

"I wore my hair in a bun, you know. How could she propose that? I was in shock. I just could not imagine such a thing. She kept working on me and working on me. 'I'm telling you this is *it!*' she said. 'There is so much money up there and it's so simple. All you have to do is get up in

*"This whole thing of go-go dancers was a new craze. Everyone sashayed into the Billiken to check out the girl scene. It was like lightning. It had just started and people couldn't believe there were actually **dancing girls**."*

*"The beauty and grace with which you live each day, that's a real important thing. You can't just go crashing through life eating sardines out of a can," says Joan, standing at the gate of her magnificent flower garden at Bird Creek. (Nan Elliot)*

front of two billion men and dance.'

"I had never danced in my life. I'd never even been in a bar. I used to go down to the Rathskeller in Seattle and drink pitchers of beer and sing German songs. That was very daring.

"She finally convinced me this was the thing to do. She called the bar where she had worked and told them she had this great dancer from San Francisco. Set me right up. It was the Billiken Lounge in Fairbanks. It was 1966, before they found oil. They were still into gold then.

"I was absolutely petrified out of my wits because of the dancing part of it. It was so out of char-

acter for me, I could not imagine. Fortunately, I didn't have to sing. All I had to do was figure out what numbers on the jukebox would suit my movements and then get with the program.

"I decided I had to look like a million bucks. So I was running and eating two tablespoons of yogurt a day and a few seeds. I was going to be a physical specimen.

"Then I set my needle to work making costumes the size of postage stamps. You know, micro-surgery. Tiny things that looked terrific. I did all these things to try and bolster my confidence, because, shoot, I was dressed like a goddamned Quaker. I was so scared. I took a couple of slugs of whiskey one night to see how that made you feel and that was definitely a good medicine. The first night I had to dance, I thought, that's it. I'm going to have two shots of whiskey. I wanted something real concentrated."

When Joan landed in Fairbanks, the news spread from bar to bar like wildfire: "New Girl In Town! Big-Time Dancer From San Francisco!"

"This whole thing of go-go dancers was a new craze. Everyone sashayed into the Billiken to check out the girl scene. It was like lightning. It had just started and people couldn't believe there were actually *dancing girls*. The bar was dark and very intimate. The men were mostly young and full of life, soldiers or gold miners. It wasn't depressing."

Just terrifying.

The music started up. Joan tossed back two shots of whiskey. The lights flashed on, the jukebox rolled out one of her special numbers, and the bartender yelled, "IT'S JOANIE! SHE'S FROM SAN FRANCISCO!"

"I had on this Chinese satin dress—postage-stamp size, of course—and black lace underwear. This was my other scheme. I wore fancy underclothes, which was considered totally bold,

*Joan welcomes visitors to her cabin in the wilderness, 1989.* (Nan Elliot)

> *"I really love music. But I have lived here in silence for so long that I know I can be without it. The birds and the wind, that's it. I don't even have electricity."*

'cause you could see right through them. The other girls had the same scant amount of clothes, but they were beach girls from California with bikinis on."

Joan took them by storm.

"Oh god. Oh, they were thrilled. Oh, geez, they said, she doesn't wear any make-up. Now that was the kind of thing that set me apart. The girl fresh out of the shower. They liked this. So I was just a smash hit after the first number. That was great, 'cause I didn't have to drink whiskey anymore. I saw they weren't going to eat me alive. I could talk to them. They were human. I'm basically terribly outgoing and friendly. They were excited and eager to talk. So this was kind of nice.

"Then all of a sudden, there's a call at the bar: 'THE SMOKE JUMPERS ARE COMING!' Which sort of meant 'Uh-oh, batten down the hatches, anything could happen.'

"The smoke jumpers strode in the back door and I saw this one blonde head glowing in the doorway. And oh—wow—he looked terrific. He looked real different than anyone else who was in there. He had this nice big smile.

"He just looked right in my eyes and said, 'Hi, what's your trip?'

"And I looked at him and said, 'I'm a mountain climber.'

"Of course, I was totally lying through my teeth, but I knew if I had to, I could climb one. I was sort of interested in getting this guy's attention. Boy, it worked too.

"So I said, 'What's your trip?'

"And he said, 'I'm just looking for a woman who wants to live in the woods.'

"Well, that was it," says Joan. "He picked me up after work that night, which was actually five in the morning. He was an imposing presence that warded off many situations that might not have been desirable. We fell madly in love. It was so exciting."

Chan Daniels had been a smoke jumper for 10 years when he met Joan. In many ways, he was an enigma. He never really had a serious job after they got together. Joan was always the money earner, dancing for nails and boards.

Together they built two houses in the woods. The first was the Hobbit House at Glacier Creek in Girdwood, built in a mossy grove of hemlock trees and blueberry bushes with wooden boardwalks running everywhere. "We never wanted to step on that beautiful carpet of moss. It was real, real special," remembers Joan. "But when the snow machine was invented, that's when we got out. Those snowmobiles would drive you out of heaven!"

In that winter of 1969, her girls were living with their father and going to school Outside. "I went out for their birthdays because it was terribly hard for me to be away from them," says Joan. One day in Seattle, Chan saw an ad in the paper announcing auditions for the national touring company of the Broadway musical "Hair."

"It was all about the hippie revolution, Vietnam, and free love. I had very strong and passionate feelings about all those things. I'd been dancing in Alaska for three years. I wouldn't say I was terrific, but I knew what I could get away with up here. Plus, I'd always been a singer. I sang with a light opera company when I was a teenager and I'd made quite a bit of money singing for weddings.

"So I could sing and I could dance now. I auditioned on a whim. Every hippie who'd ever picked up a guitar was there."

Out of hundreds, 32 were chosen. Joan was one of them.

"Being with theater people was very exciting. They're so spontaneous and so terribly talented. At a moment's notice, they could do anything. I really liked that. It was like, for the first time,

*Joan as the "White Swing" in the national touring company of the Broadway musical "Hair" in 1971.* (Joan Daniels Collection)

I was really with my own kind. Usually, I'm sticking out a little bit.

"'Hair' had a strong message and the music was so beautiful. It dealt mostly with the war, growing up, the confusion of feelings, and the looser sexual freedom. All the major issues of the '60s.

"But it's the nude scene that

people have never forgotten. In those days, it was quite shocking. Of course, it wasn't anything to me after dancing up here for so long. The scene was artfully done. The lights were so beautiful and subdued. The music was nice.

"I will never forget the Wednesday matinees in Miami. All the matrons would come. Just as the nude scene unfolded, the

*"I will never forget the Wednesday matinees in Miami. All the matrons would come. Just as the nude scene unfolded, the whole audience would lift up and focus their opera glasses all in unison, and we would just roar."*

whole audience would lift up and focus their opera glasses all in unison, and we would just roar," she says, breaking into wild laughter at the memory.

"For young people, we were celebrities. There's no doubt about it."

When Joan returned to Alaska, she proposed to friends the idea of buying land in common, specifically 20 acres bordering Chugach State Park on the banks of Bird Creek.

"The idea was to share the expense of the land and get out to the wilderness instantly. This was like the ultimate, idealistic, hippie fantasy. Everybody jumped on it. Oh, boy! We all just came leaping out here, popped up our tents, and thrashed out our scenes. The joints were passed around for years until some of us got out of smoking. When the smoke cleared, we found we had more than a few differences, socially and intellectually. But I still feel it was a great way to have a piece of land developed."

Joan's younger daughter, Sara, vividly remembers her first trips to Alaska. Most of their school years, she and Scarlet lived with their father in Washington. But summers, they came up to stay with this "wild radical hippie" who was their mom.

"Dad is not a straight arrow, but he is conservative," says Sara. "Mom would always send us photos of her lounging in her go-go outfits. And Dad was cool. He wouldn't say word one. So, we thought Mom was groovy. Here she was on a wolf skin rug in tiny sequined outfits and dangling earrings. We were so proud of her.

"We first came to Alaska when I was 11, dressed in little sailor suits. Then we came back the summer I was 14. Mom had just bought the Bird Creek property. Some hippies led us down the hill and across the bridge. Mom was standing with Chan on the other side of the boardwalk.

"All she could do was look at us and go, 'Oh my god, oh my god . . .'

"We were so high school-y. We went from being little girls to teenagers. We had on gold eye shadow, eye liner, and my eyebrows were plucked to the hilt. They were little strings. We had on some polyester outfit and high heels. She hadn't seen us in three years and the first thing she tried to do was grow my eyebrows back. Every morning I woke up, rushed to the mirror and groaned. I was living in a tent. 'They're growing back beautifully, dear,' she'd say. I'd groan and say, 'They're *so ugly!*'"

Sara, who is 30 and now living in Anchorage, is definitely a chip off the old block with the same funny and animated storytelling style as her mother.

"Mom started right in on the manners. Even though she lives in the woods and she doesn't have a toilet, she has manners. That's one of the most important things in the whole world to my mother. It shows you have respect for somebody else and yourself. Mom has a way of telling a story at the top of her lungs that's funny, outrageous, bawdy, and silly, but she still has manners.

"Man, that woman would make us work! That's one of the greatest things we got from our mom, loving hard work. Being with her brought out all our theatrical qualities and singing. We would sing all the time.

"Living at Bird Creek was great. You could go for walks in the woods and pick wildflowers. Mom loves flowers and her garden is gorgeous. She has a lot of guests like bear and moose and coyote. As kids, we used to swim in the ponds with the salmon. Honest to god! It was freezing cold. We'd open our eyes underwater and just swim upstream with them. One of our favorite things was to pick spruce tips for spruce tip tea. We dried everything—mushrooms, spruce tips, gallons of cranberries, blueberries, raspberries—everything

*Joan, her daughter Sara Eickmeyer, and Joan's three grandchildren, Venek, Nathan, and Lupine. (Nan Elliot)*

*"Living at Bird Creek was great. Mom has a lot of guests like bear and moose and coyote. As kids, we used to swim in the ponds with the salmon. Honest to god! It was freezing cold. We'd open our eyes underwater and just swim upstream with them."*

—Sara Eickmeyer

you could gather from the woods to eat, to drink, to sleep on. My mom lives in a great place and she encouraged all the wonderful things you could get out of that place. She never said 'no.'

"We went to see her dance in Seward at The Flamingo or 'The Flaming O' as they called it. That was a big thrill. Chan took us. She looked beautiful with her long brown hair and the green sequined outfits and the flashing lights. We thought this was the living end. She'd show up all her great moves and the guys would yell, 'Ohhhh, Joanie!' She just loved it. My mom really likes to entertain people, to make people laugh.

"Her best friends in Seward were old man Andrew and this ancient woman named Lila who looked a little like Lucille Ball and thought she was still living in the 1920s. Lila owned the second-hand store. Mom spent her nights with the guys in the bars, getting tips, and making money so she could raise everybody, buy the land, get the lumber, and pay off her truck. But her days were spent with these beautiful old people who had a lot to offer her. And that's what she enjoyed, being with these quality people."

Joan's years as a dancer took her through a wild ride of humanity. After Fairbanks, she danced in a sleazy part of Fourth Avenue in downtown Anchorage.

"They had just the roughest, toughest characters around. I saw things in there I'll probably never see again. Hard living people who were terribly aggressive and cruel to one another. And bartenders who were ripping off Native people. Just the worst lowlife you could imagine. I tell you, there were many nights I didn't sleep thinking about what I'd seen. When you see your fellow human beings and see what they're capable of doing to each other, I think it's a good thing to know. The potential is there in all of us. When you see inhumanity, it's real impressive. And it's lower than animal. You don't see animals treat each other like that. I was grateful I had the guts to stick that little session out.

"I was vulnerable! There were many times my dressing room door was like a shower curtain. They would just beat that thing to splinters. If someone wasn't watching me and every move I made, I was really in danger. A lot of times, I had behemoths come through my door like it was cheesecloth. And they'd be on me physically."

Joan lasted there about three months and then went to the little fishing town of Seward on Resurrection Bay where she danced for three years. As she says, "We needed more nails."

"Those were the years king crab was still king!" remembers Joan. "Those fishermen were the hardest working people. They lived on the life and death edge of their work. They were great. I loved them. Those guys used to bring me gunnysacks of shelled scallops—scallops the size of pie plates—and just throw them on the stage while I was dancing. I would have huge king salmon and king crab flopping around, still alive, at my feet. I mean, those guys brought me *everything!*

"I used to have a friend down there in Seward—Lila Larsen. She was in her 80s. A walking antique. She was a tough girl. She ran her own dog team for many years. She taught me so many things. The last year she was alive, I carried her every place on my back. I'd carry her up the side of the mountain 'cause she wanted to show me where these special mushrooms grew. I learned more from her than anyone. She was funny! 'I can catch more fish on a safety pin than those guys can catch with all their fancy gear,' she'd say. And she could, too!

"Lila was kind of a mysterious person. She really liked me 'cause I liked wild things. We had a lot of fun together. I swear

to god, she was so old, how she would do these things!" Joan shakes her head, laughing at the memory.

"One day, Lila drove up a mountain road and saw this bear. She promptly got her gun and ripped out of the car and shot that thing.

"And I said, 'Good god, Lila, how'd you get that thing in the car to take it home?'

"She said, 'Kid, I had an *awful* time getting that thing in the car.'"

Joan laughs, still in amazement. "I mean, she was no bigger than a mosquito, you know. A tiny, frail, old person—my god!"

Joan Daniels has lived her dream with a gutsiness and graciousness that would be hard to match. "I'm a wild thing, that's for sure. It can't be helped," she says with a kind of coquettishness, fluttering her eyelids, and then breaking into a merry infectious laugh.

"I really treasure the old ways of doing things. For me, to make moose mincemeat in the fall—I can't face skipping it. It's part of the ritual of life. Food and flowers and berries, that's the rhythm of life that I really appreciate. I couldn't live in a place that doesn't have wild foods growing. I'm a gatherer. In spring, I always go down to the mouth of the creek and gather wild greens, sour-

*"I really treasure the old ways of doing things. For me, to make moose mincemeat in the fall—I can't face skipping it. It's part of the ritual of life. Food and flowers and berries, that's the rhythm of life that I really appreciate. I couldn't live in a place that doesn't have wild foods growing. I'm a gatherer."*

*Joan taps the birch trees in spring to make a very special kind of birch syrup.* (Nan Elliot)

When it's fall, it's glorious. In spring come all the birds, all the thrushes. They're singing some kind of Mozart. I love bird songs in the spring. They're performing their operas, their little romances are flourishing."

It's not easy to get to Joan's house despite her proximity to civilization. Over the mountains from Anchorage in Bird Creek valley, her home lies half a treacherous mile from the road, by foot. First, it's down a steep, rutted icy hill, sometimes hanging onto the cranberry roots for dear life. Then, you follow a little jeep trail past a few cabins across the creek over a heavy wood bridge of warped planks which have survived five floods.

Down a dark trail overgrown with alders, you climb up onto a 120-foot steel-cable suspension bridge that swings 15 feet above the rushing waters of Bird Creek. On the other side, the path leads into a thicket of willows often hiding a moose or a bear. Then it goes over the boardwalk, past the rabbit house, the salmon pond, and the woodshed with five years' supply of wood and into a spectacular garden of flowers, berries, and vegetables. Joan's two-story home, built of rough lumber and ringed with porches, sits on the boundary of Chugach State Park.

dock, and mushrooms. I tap the birch trees for sap and boil it down for syrup. In the fall, I snatch berries from their mothers and put them to sleep for winter jewels. Berries are my bank account. These things I felt when I was really young, and they haven't let me down one little bit.

"I really love music, too. But I have lived here in silence for so long that I know I can be without it. The birds and the wind, that's it. I don't even have electricity. For 15 years, we only had candles. Now we have propane lights.

"In this particular house (it is hexagonal with windows on all sides), every season is a wonder. It's like living in a weather bowl.

Every board and bolt and square inch of dirt is precious. She has literally danced for every nail and, more often than not, dragged the lumber there herself.

"Joan Daniels is the strongest woman I know," says Doug Fesler, a big, blonde, bearded mountain man, once a Bird Creek neighbor and former back-country ranger.

Joan grins when she hears that. "That's something coming from him," she says, clearly pleased. And then with her fast wit, she laughs and jokes, "It's also because he's never busted me, and he's probably tried hard."

"Busted" here does not mean drugs or booze. It means bears.

Joan has shot several marauding black bears and one notorious grizzly that was terrorizing Bird Creek valley. It was all in self-defense (and out of season). When the grizzly bit the dust, the news was hot all up and down the highway: "Joan Daniels shot the grizzly!" Game wardens tromped over the creek and up to her property looking for the carcass. A bear shot out of season must be turned over to the authorities.

"Damn near got busted on that one," says Joan. "You see, you can shoot for self-protection, but you can't keep it. And that pissed me off. It's a hell of a lot of trouble to be confronted by a bear and

have to destroy it. I made use of everything. I skinned him out. I hung him up. I butchered him and I ate him. And they wanted to come and take him, probably to auction off the hide and toe-nails at their Christmas party and throw the meat away.

"I tell you what. I ate that bear. But I'd never eat another grizzly. It's not tasty meat. I ended up making him completely into sausage. I felt very strongly about not wasting anything."

It was the middle of a spring day. Joan's mother was visiting from Washington. Joan thought she saw a moose in the garden. Then, all of a sudden, a big grizzly came roaring at full speed for the house, leaped up on the porch, and started bashing his paws against the windows to get in. Joan tried to shout him down. Her poor dear mother was wringing every handkerchief in the house to shreds.

Cautiously, Joan opened the porthole in the front door, shoved the rifle out, and shot six inches from the bear's head. That was merely an annoyance. He returned, minutes later, charging 40 miles an hour onto the porch and began throwing everything around.

"I said to my mother, 'This is it. I've got to do something.' I went to the upstairs porch.

*When the grizzly bit the dust, the news was hot all up and down the highway: "Joan Daniels shot the grizzly!"*

*Grizzly.* (National Park Service)

"I knew my shot had to be deadly or he would tear this house apart. I shot him in the shoulder. He clawed the air for a while and then died. Quickly, I shoved a pan under him to catch the blood so there wouldn't be a mess. I sure didn't want any of his relatives coming around smelling his blood. Then, I lifted him into the wheelbarrow and pushed him over to the animal house.

"The Fish and Game wardens came here, but I eluded them. Little kids in the valley saw them coming and warned me.

"I quickly ran over and got that bear out of the animal house, stuffed him in the wheelbarrow, roared back to the house at 90 miles an hour, put him on my back, and hauled the whole goddamn thing up the ladder to the second story, threw him on the bedroom floor, slammed the trap door shut, and came back down. They never could catch me because I'd been so damn careful.

"That was a nightmare. Those guys kept coming around for weeks. I slept with that bear, butchered it, and packed it out of here. I took it into town to a friend's house, threw all her stuff out of the freezer, stuffed the bear in, and jammed her stuff back on top, so she'd never know it was there.

"A few weeks later, she called and said, 'Joan, did you leave a whole bunch of packages in our freezer labeled *BB King*?'" Joan grins proudly. BB stands for brown bear.

This was not Joan's first intimate experience with bears. The year she and Chan got together, they worked for a season assisting a big game guide in the Wrangell Mountains and out on the Alaska Peninsula. Joan was the camp cook and one of the chief bear skinners.

"Fleshing out bear hides and having to sleep in the tent with a stack of them six-foot deep was kind of a new experience. I did that for a season and sure learned about big game hunters. Amazing mentality. It's just EGO with capital letters. They have a very warped view of nature and wild animals. The whole thing of big game hunting is built on a tape measure. How big are the horns? How big is that rack? If they shot something and it wasn't the right size, we'd just have to fly off and find another one. In those days, there weren't any regulations. Well, they were there on the books. But nobody paid any attention to them, because there was no work crew to enforce them.

"Those big game guides were just rampaging. It was horrible. It was another one of those things that would keep me from sleeping at night.

"I'm not sad about animals dying one bit, because I'm a meat eater. But the mentality of killing this thing only for the trophy, *that* was *enraging*. It's just not right, period. There's no integrity there at all. None.

"All the hunters ever did was pull the trigger. While the guide is doing all this terrible, ferocious hard work getting these beasts and their hides and their horns back to camp, the hunter would be having cocktails. He doesn't have a drop of blood on him. He's got on this brand new outfit. After you lug that thing back to camp, then he asks if you'll hoist the horns onto his back so he can have his photo made. Boy, I tell you, it's real different. That was a profession I was glad I did once and would never ever be a party to twice.

"Every spare moment out there, I would be picking berries. With cloths strung up in trees, I strained berries all over camp. Of course, the hunters wouldn't eat anything like that. No way. If it wasn't out of a jar, forget it. Every blooming day, they'd have to be flown in to some place with a telephone so they could check on the stock market. Sometimes, you'd be standing out on the dirt runway at night with lanterns and candles so the pilot could land just so these suckers could find out what was happening on Wall Street. Neurotic, screwed up mess, these men were. I couldn't believe it. Always too, it seemed they were bigots. Never found a person with a wholesome attitude towards other humans. All this twisted, hateful prejudice. I swear to god, that was worse than the Fourth Avenue scene. These people had money. They were educated. Yet they were still lowlifes. Of course, there would be the exception. But not many."

For two years, Joan and Chan lived in an army tent in Bird Creek as they built their house around them on the tent platform. Sometimes, it got so cold that even Joan's clothes would freeze and then break in half when she tried to put them on. After slogging through the mud and the woods and the creek in her hip boots to go dancing every night for seven years, Joan finally retired her sequined postage stamps in 1974 only to get sucked into the restaurant and catering business nearly 24 hours a day. Her cooking is legendary.

"The beauty and grace with which you meet each day, that's a real important thing. You can't just go crashing through life eating sardines out of a can," says

*"Alaska is my real husband. It's the call of the mountains. People hear the word 'Alaska' and it's magic all over the world."*

*Joan walks home over the suspension bridge she built herself, which spans the rapids of Bird Creek. (Nan Elliot)*

Joan as she stirs her birch sap syrup over the fire. The aroma is light and sweet.

"In order to live the kind of life I live, you've got to be a healthy person and you must be physically strong. You have to be adaptable, because so many things happen in a week that are so extreme and can really knock you for a loop. You really are living here almost totally by the weather. The weather is your dictator. One thing I notice that seems to be universal in people living in contemporary society is the complaint about the weather. It's constant. If it's not a perfectly blue sunny day—yuck!

"To me, weather is really the last frontier. This is the last thing left. Even a mountain we can blow up or denude. But the weather, that's the real show going on. I try to impress that on the little children who come here.

"'Jo Jo, you don't have television,' they will say. 'Hey, go out and look at the sky. That's the real television,' I tell them. The kids get sort of interested. Here, the weather is moving so fast. Then, I'll look out and say, 'Uh-oh, the channel changed.' And they'll run outside. 'Hey, Jo Jo,' they yell, 'the channel changed. You were right.'

"The romance of the weather has really been taken away from people. Everyone likes to take a shower, but if the earth gets a shower, people can't handle it. They try to put something between themselves and the weather. That's what makes the earth the earth.

"I've been away from Bird Creek for many months now and last night I walked in here in the dark and the rain. The damp brings out all the smells I know and love. Even the rotting fish on the banks.

"Alaska is my real husband. It's the call of the mountains.

"People hear the word 'Alaska,' and it's magic all over the world. It just seems to get everybody's imagination stirred up."

# 6

# The Grand Old Man
# Of The Iditarod

J oe Redington, Sr., that sly old fox, is a legend in his
own time.

In 1979, at age 62, never having climbed a mountain over 5,000 feet, he mushed his dog team up to the
summit of Mt. McKinley, North America's highest and
coldest mountain.

As the father of the Iditarod Sled Dog Race—a
thousand-mile mushing marathon through the heart of the
Alaska wilderness—Joe not only started the race, chris-
tened it, and raised money for it, but also for the past 16
years has raced in it.

He's 72 years old today and still racing.

Alaskans just shake their heads and grin. Joe
Redington defines that old slogan: "When the going gets
tough, the tough get going."

Redington has plunged himself and his dog team
through thin ice into freezing rivers; frostbitten his hands
and feet camping out on the trail in weather where the

*Joe Redington, Sr., defines that old slogan: "When the going gets tough, the tough get going."* (Paul Brown, Anchorage Daily News)

temperature with wind-chill factor was 130 degrees below zero; gotten sick with pneumonia; and still, he's mushed on. Once he had to drop out before the beginning of the race. ("A moose tromped me. Broke some ribs. Banged up my knee and leg. I couldn't run.") Four times along the trail he's had to scratch before reaching the coast of the frozen Bering Sea. ("Dropped into a hole outside of Shaktoolik. Collapsed one lung. Broke some ribs. I was pretty battered up. Had to fly into Nome. Things like that is why I've scratched.") But 10 times, Joe Redington has finished in the money, one of the top 20. Four times he was in fifth place.

In 1988, at the age of 71, he led the pack of 50 mushers for much of the race. He felt, he said grinning, like "an old fox pursued by 50 young hounds."

To Alaskans, Joe Redington is best, most affectionately, and sometimes even reverently known as the "Father of the Iditarod." But he has worn many different hats in his lifetime. A former paratrooper, parachuter, and pilot, he rarely gets excited over danger. ("I don't scare very easy.") But he has sure scared other people.

All of Alaska has held its collective breath at least twice when Redington disappeared in his plane somewhere over the vast untraveled wilderness . . . and breathed a sigh of relief when, after much jury-rigging and numerous crash landings, a sheepish Joe Redington limped his plane home, always surprised and slightly embarrassed over the gush of publicity and concern about his welfare.

To meet this man, one expects a robust Paul Bunyan character, bigger than life. But he fools you. He is a small man with a soft voice. His ruggedness and strength are not immediately impressive. What is striking is his gentleness.

Joe Redington's life, even before he reached Alaska, is like a tale spun from an old nickelodeon. It was fast-paced, eventful, adventurous, daring, and daredevil. When they say it cannot be done, it's a challenge he accepts with single-minded determination.

His daddy rode a horse into Oklahoma seven years before that land was made a state. He was a homesteader and later a railroad man. But he loved to travel. Although he was a respectable man himself, he seemed to have had a soft spot in his heart for those who walked on the far side of the law.

Oklahoma at the turn of the century was known as Outlaw Country.

Joe's mother? Well, it is ru-

*Joe Redington's life, even before he reached Alaska, is like a tale spun from an old nickelodeon. It was fast-paced, eventful, adventurous, daring, and daredevil. When they say it cannot be done, it's a challenge he accepts with single-minded determination.*

*Joe Redington, Sr., mushing down Fourth Avenue in Anchorage at the start of the 1,000-mile Iditarod Sled Dog Race.* (*Erik Hill,* Anchorage Daily News)

mored down in those parts that she was the daughter of the notorious Belle Starr, the "Bandit Queen," a "Female Jesse James."

When Joe and his brother, Ray, were very little, their mother disappeared one day, just kind of rode off into the sunset . . . maybe after her latest bank robbery, admits Joe with an amused twin-kle in his eye. His father refused to ever speak of her again.

"Even when I joined the Army, I wasn't sure of my mother's maiden name. I had to make one up. One time I'd call it Mackintosh. Then I'd forget that and call it something else. Later, I found out evidently it was Smith . . . maybe . . . if that wasn't some sort of alias," says Joe.

One day, about four years ago, Joe received a phone call from a tourist at Mt. McKinley National Park.

"Are you Joe Redington?" asked the tourist.

"Yes," Joe said.

"I'm your brother."

"Well, I don't think so," Joe answered calmly.

"Yes," the man continued. "There are four of us. We all live in Oklahoma."

"When he got home," says Joe, "he sent me a newspaper clipping describing where my mother had left him and the other three children stranded on a street corner in Enid, Oklahoma. Just left them there and walked off. This was a group she had before I was born, before she married my dad. I didn't even know about them until I was pretty near 70 years old.

"I guess if the U.S. marshal was chasing you, you might even have to leave the children if you didn't want to get caught," says Joe with that soft grin. "Maybe that's what happened in Enid, Oklahoma. I don't know.

"My dad did remarry . . . to another outlaw." Joe shakes his head with a kind of bemused look. "I don't know how he found all those damn outlaws. This one was Evelyn Montgomery. I recall going to McAlester penitentiary to visit her brother. He was in jail for bank robbery. Another of her brothers lived with us, even after my dad got rid of her. She was too wild, I guess. The brother who lived with us was named L.J. He was just a kid, 14 or 15 years old. Clavis Montgomery was the

*"When I was 11 years old, my dad bought a farm down in southeastern Oklahoma. It was 1928. It was not uncommon at all to see a bank with a sign on it: 'This bank closed, robbed by Pretty Boy Floyd.'"*

one who was in jail for robbing a bank. When Clavis got out on parole, he got hold of L.J. and robbed another bank and killed the cashier. The last I heard of them, they were both serving 'life' in McAlester, Oklahoma.

"You see, until statehood, the only law in Oklahoma was the United States marshals and they were real scarce. So every person wanted by the law anywhere in the United States fled to Oklahoma when they opened up that territory. There were good people as well—frontiers people—hundreds of them to one of the bad ones. But in eastern Oklahoma, the people were poor.

"Outlaws considered the people they robbed as the ones who could afford it. People like Pretty Boy Floyd was respected more than the president of the United States to the Okies. They stole from the rich and gave to the poor and it made heroes out of them.

"When I was 11 years old, my

dad bought a farm down in southeastern Oklahoma. It was 1928. It was not uncommon at all to see a bank with a sign on it: 'This bank closed, robbed by Pretty Boy Floyd.'

"I remember one robbery very clearly. We was living about 30 miles from Hugo, Oklahoma. Pretty Boy Floyd rode into town in a Packard touring car, fired a few shots up and down the street, walked into the bank at Hugo, took the money, went out, got into his Packard car, and drove off. Then pretty soon the sheriff showed up. That's exactly what happened. All Pretty Boy had to do was fire a few rounds up and down the street with his machine gun and he had no problems. The town was his.

"In the early days of my life, I was associated with all these outlaws and bank robbers and such, but my dad took good care of us. He never let Ray or me get into any trouble with the law and we traveled all over the United States. He was honest to a fault. I guess he'd been around so many outlaws that he kind of went the other way. It never rubbed off on my brother or me. Neither one of us even smoked or drank, although my dad did plenty of both.

"One thing my dad was very strong on was your word.

"He said, 'The only thing that amounts to anything is a person's word. Once you lose that, you're done.' So there was never any lying. That's one thing I can't stand. I tell the truth even if it hurts me. I don't think anyone on this earth could ever say that I told them an outright lie. I don't believe in that."

The Roaring '20s were quickly followed by the Great Depression. By 1929, Joe's dad, always a traveling man, had pulled up stakes again and took his two sons on the road.

Like characters out of John Steinbeck's *Grapes of Wrath*, they were the "Okies" on the move. They worked the wheat harvest in Minnesota, branded turkeys in Wyoming, drove a combine in Washington, picked prunes and hops in the Pacific Northwest, and picked peaches, dates, and cotton in California.

"You could make a dollar a day if you worked hard," remembers Joe. "But things got real bad down there in California. People were actually starving to death. It was the height of the Depression.

"On Christmas Day one year we had oatmeal for breakfast. No milk, just a little sugar. For Christmas dinner, we had the same thing, only we added a little chocolate to it. And on Christmas Day!" he repeats with indignation. "It was time to leave that country. So we sold the Chrysler car for 13 dollars, made a profit of a dollar on it, and went and caught the freight train.

"I remember well one of the brakemen on the train yelling, 'Get in the car there and if one of you damn Okies sticks your head out I'm gonna knock it off with the lantern.'"

Dodging "railroad bulls," they jumped freight trains and rode thousands of miles. But security got tighter and Joe remembers one cold ride out of Amarillo, Texas, when one of the railroad detectives spotted them. They leaped onto one of the tank cars just as the train was pulling out. The detective leaped on after them. It was a scene out of an old slapstick comedy. They ran 'round and 'round the little platform on the tank car just out of grasp of the detective panting behind them, until finally as the train picked up speed, he had to leap off.

At one point they got hooked up with some Irish gypsies in Indiana who were involved in a peculiar moneymaking racket.

"The girls sold handkerchiefs and flower baskets and the old man and the boys sold 'fresh country butter.' You couldn't get away with it these days, but this was 1930," says Joe with a grin.

*(Bob Hallinen,* Anchorage Daily News*)*

*Because of his love for dogs, challenge, and adventure, Joe Redington has done what others dreamed impossible. He struggled against enormous skepticism to create the Iditarod Sled Dog Race in 1973, the thousand-mile marathon through bitter extremes of country and weather, a race that would test the mettle of men, women, and dogs alike, an adventure befitting the last frontier.*

"That butter deal was the damndest thing I'd ever seen. The old man would mix up a tub of 'butter' each night. He put some kind of powders in it, and, hell, it looked and tasted just like butter. Only you didn't dare put it on a hot biscuit. It would be just like you dipped it in a bucket of water. So we'd have to sell it real quick and get the heck out of town, before the cops ran us out."

Redington started for Alaska in 1934, got as far as Seattle, but couldn't raise the $34 for the boat to Skagway. He finally made it 11 years later after World War II, joined by his father, his brother Ray, and Ray's wife Vi. (After Ray departed, Vi married Joe.)

At the border, someone gave them a little husky puppy. And that's how it all started—a lifelong passion for dogs.

Joe homesteaded in Knik, directly north from Anchorage across the Knik Arm of Cook Inlet; ran a lodge out at Flathorn Lake; did some guiding and commercial fishing; and with his dogs joined the Air Force Mountain Rescue, salvaging wreckage and picking up any survivors from plane crashes into Mount Susitna. In those days, that low mountain, a distinctive landmark on the Anchorage horizon, often known as "The Sleeping Lady," was a treacherous obstacle for planes flying in bad weather without instrument warnings.

One summer day in 1968, Joe and Vi were commercial fishing at the mouth of the Susitna River, loading the boat with salmon for a trip back to port, when a young Swiss fellow crawled on board and asked if he could ride in with them. He introduced himself as Ray Genet.

"We finally figured out who he was—the guy who had made the first winter ascent of Mt. McKinley the year before," recounts Joe. "So Vi took the controls and I went out on the deck and talked to Ray. By the time we got to Anchorage, we had already made a deal to go up the mountain the next summer. I asked him if he thought we could make it to the summit with dogs and he thought so, so I said, 'OK, I want to go.'"

That trip would be postponed and delayed for 11 years until the spring of 1979. Redington and a young mushing friend, Susan Butcher, who had originally trained under Joe (and by 1988 would be a three-time champion of the Iditarod Sled Dog Race), had just finished racing their dog teams a thousand miles to Nome. It was Redington's sixth Iditarod race. Both he and Susan were ready and eager to assault Mt. McKinley.

In those intervening years, Ray Genet was also making history. He had climbed and led teams to the summit of Alaska's most famous mountain nearly 30 times before the "Mt. McKinley Sled Dog Expedition" got underway.

However, at the last minute, Genet determined that the mountain was too dangerous for dogs that year. There were too many avalanches and too many crevasses. Genet was reluctant to accept responsibility as leader. Instead, he took the role of adviser to the dog mushers and would guide them over the most difficult places to the summit, in between leading other expeditions on the mountain. (It was to be Genet's last summer on McKinley. In October of that year, he died on a bivouac while descending from the summit of Mt. Everest in Nepal.)

So Joe, who had never been higher than the top of Mt. Susitna at 4,400 feet, took charge as leader of the group. The mushers spent 44 days on the mountain. They battled winds up to 100 miles an hour and temperatures that dropped to 40 below zero. They broke three dog sleds and had to leave one team of dogs and several members of the expedition at 14,000 feet. In some places, they were just hanging on the side of the mountain. One misplaced step and they could have tumbled thousands of feet.

"Susan and I both tied into the dogs, but Genet never would. He felt there was too much chance that they could go over a cliff," says Joe, going on to describe how surprised other climbers were to meet a dog team on the mountain.

"In steep places, the dogs were too hard to handle. That was our only problem. They had just come off the Iditarod and they were ready to go. The altitude never bothered them a bit. They loved it. I had veterinarians tell me the dogs couldn't make it that high. Every once in a while they got nervous, because they didn't like looking down several

*So Joe, who had never been higher than the top of Mt. Susitna at 4,400 feet, took charge as leader of the Mt. McKinley Sled Dog Expedition. The mushers spent 44 days on the mountain. They battled winds up to 100 miles an hour and temperatures that dropped to 40 below zero.*

*Joe mushes to the summit of Mt. McKinley, the highest and coldest mountain in North America at 20,320 feet. (Rob Stapleton)*

thousand feet. But the dogs were barking at the summit, ready to go higher."

Because of his love for dogs, challenge, and adventure, Joe Redington has done what others dreamed impossible. He struggled against enormous skepticism to create the Iditarod Sled Dog Race in 1973, the thousand-mile marathon through bitter extremes of country and weather, a race that would test the mettle of men, women, and dogs alike, an adventure befitting the last frontier.

The name "Iditarod" comes from the name of an old gold town, hastily built around the turn of the century in a mosquito-infested swamp that was bad even by Alaska standards. It was part of an inland empire of gold in Alaska that boomed from 1909 to 1917.

There were two routes to Iditarod in those early days. The longer, but easier one, was to take the overland trail in the summer from Valdez to Fairbanks, float 540 miles by steamer down the Yukon River and then wind 400 sluggish miles along the incredibly tedious Innoko and Iditarod Rivers to the gold camp of Iditarod. The alternative winter route was shorter, but far more treacherous, passing through two mountain ranges in formidable weather. This was the sled dog trail used for carrying mail and supplies 600 miles from the little town of Seward on the coast of the North Pacific Ocean to Iditarod in the interior.

On the maps of the old mail carriers that route through the interior was known as the "Seward to Nome Trail" which connected an ice-free port on the Pacific Ocean with the historic gold rush

(Photos by Rob Stapleton.)

Joe Redington stands with his dog team on the summit of Mt. McKinley, May 28, 1979. The expedition also included Susan Butcher, who by 1988 would be a three-time champion of the Iditarod, photographer Rob Stapleton, and the legendary Swiss-Alaskan mountaineering guide Ray "Pirate" Genet.

"In steep places, the dogs were too hard to handle. That was our only problem. They had just come off the Iditarod and they were ready to go. The altitude never bothered them a bit. They loved it. I had veterinarians tell me the dogs couldn't make it that high. Every once in a while they got nervous, because they didn't like looking down several thousand feet. But the dogs were barking at the summit, ready to go higher."

Ray "Pirate" Genet.

town of Nome on the Bering Sea. A short spur along that route that led into the gold town was called the "Iditarod Trail."

When that inland empire of gold collapsed, that short trail fell into disuse and Iditarod quickly became a ghost town.

But the ghost of Iditarod did not slip quietly into history.

In 1973—thanks to Joe Redington—the golden name of "Iditarod" became the romantic and popular name for a thousand miles of that old mail trail stretching from Anchorage to Nome.

Today, Iditarod is synonymous in Alaska and around the world with the longest and most arduous dog mushing race in history. Every year in March, mushers test their courage in some of the most extreme conditions on the face of the globe to compete for title of champion.

But the battle to establish the race was not easily won.

A long-distance race over wilderness terrain was a different concept for Alaskans, until then only accustomed to sprint racing for dogs. Redington was nicknamed in the newspapers as "The Don Quixote of Alaska"— the dreamer. Critics said it was impractical, a farce. They couldn't believe this crazy guy Redington was going to run a race with no money and no support. They felt surely the dogs would starve to death and the whole thing would be a disaster. The mushers gave him the worst time of all, he says. Even they didn't think dogs had the stamina to make it all the way to Nome.

Joe had promised $50,000 prize money for the finishers in Nome, but the night before the race, there wasn't a dime in the bank, which didn't lend to his credibility.

Before the start of the race at the mushers' banquet, Joe gave the best speech he's ever given, says his wife, Vi, a warm-hearted little lady, whose life motto in this daredevil family is "Try Not To Worry." Joe promised the money would be waiting for them at the finish line. Even though he trained his dogs for the race, he stayed behind to fly support of food and supplies for the other mushers on the trail. In two weeks, he also raised $51,000 and made good on his promise.

By popularizing long-distance dog racing, Joe Redington has brought dogs back to Alaska.

"The damn snow machines were coming in and the dogs were disappearing," says the senior musher. "When I went out to villages where there were beautiful dogs once, a snow machine was sitting in front of a house and no dogs. That wasn't good. I didn't like that. I've seen snow machines

*"I just can't say 'no' to a dog. What money I have, I spend on my dogs. I could be smoking, drinking, and running around with wild women—spend my money that way— but I just dog it."*

(*Bob Hallinen*, Anchorage Daily News)

sled marathon through five European countries. The name of this hot new race, which started and finished in the Italian Alps, is— what else?—the Alpirod, a direct descendent of the Iditarod.

The Alpirod is not the only race born of the Iditarod.

First came the Iditaski, a long-distance cross-country ski race over 210 miles of the historic trail. Then came the Iditashoe, a mere 105-mile dash on snowshoes. In 1987 emerged the newest version, the Iditabike, with contestants bumping more than 200 miles down the winter trail on mountain bikes. So many little Idita-races have evolved that one wisecracker claims the original Iditarod is misnamed and suggests re-naming it to "Iditadog."

That'd probably be OK with the daddy of the race. After all, Joe says, the real heroes of the Iditarod are the dogs. Redington owns about 450 of them. But he's run more than 5,000 in his lifetime over 150,000 miles of wilderness. One day, he hopes to get dog mushing into the Olympics.

"I just can't say 'no' to a dog. What money I have, I spend on my dogs. I could be smoking, drinking, and running around with wild women—spend my money that way—but I just dog it," he says with a soft, endearing grin.

break down and fellows freeze to death out there in the wilderness. But dogs will always keep you warm and they'll get you there."

In 1980, Joe realized a dream. The Iditarod race route was declared a National Historic Trail by the U.S. Congress. In 16 years, the field of competitors has doubled. Mushers arrive from all over the world. Record time over the trail is nearly twice as fast, slashed from 20 days in 1973 to 11 days in 1989.

The Iditarod has been called "The Last Great Race." But, by virtue of its very existence (and with a lot of encouragement from Joe), it has inspired many other races. In January of 1988, Joe flew to Italy, all expenses paid, for the first annual 10-day, 600-mile dog

# 7

# First Homesteaders On Soldotna Creek

**M**arge Mullen grew up in the heart of Chicago, a young city girl studying to be a painter. Her life in later years proved radically different. Like her Irish ancestors, she learned to draw her strength from the land.

Newly married at the age of 24, Marge and her husband Frank flew their small plane north to Alaska. Out on the frontier, away from the bright lights of the city, Marge was amazed. "The trees were so small, the sky was so big, and you could see all the stars at night."

At that time, homesteading was only rumored to be open on the Kenai Peninsula. They settled in Anchorage temporarily. But they were really headed for distant wilderness. They picked a spot on the map, about 150 miles south of the city where a small creek flows into the blue-green glacial waters of the Kenai River. There was no road in that direction. So they took the train as far as they could go, hitched a ride along a jeep trail,

*Today, three generations of Mullens live on the homestead property. Marge Mullen, right, standing with her daughter Peggy on the banks of the Kenai River, first arrived in 1947 to stake out the land. "We had just enough for a little grubstake," she remembers. "I found out what that really meant—a few cartons of groceries and a trusty rifle."*
*(Nan Elliot)*

*Marge on her honeymoon in Florida with a boat full of admirers.*
*(Mullen Collection)*

and when the road ran out, the two city slickers from Chicago—who had never before worn packs on their backs or been out in the wilderness—walked the remaining 80 miles out of the mountains through the flatlands and the charred debris of a still-smoking forest fire to Soldotna Creek.

It took them three days of walking to get there. When they did, there was no one else for miles except a couple of bachelors down the river, a few fox farmers 14 miles south in Kasilof, and the Native villagers of Kenai 12 miles west on the coast of Cook Inlet. They were the first homesteading family to stake their claim on the creek. With their arrival began the history of settlement in Soldotna. Today, it is a town of 4,000. Three generations of Mullens now live on the homestead property.

"We had just enough for a little grubstake," remembers Marge. "I found out what that really meant—a few cartons of groceries and a trusty rifle. It was an extremely cold winter that year. With two little children, I had to have a place with a fire before I could move permanently from Anchorage. After we put in the foundations, Frank went back in February to put up the logs. I

*"The majority of homesteaders were single men," recounts Marge. "And I can say that for the first time in my life, I really missed the companionship of other women. The bachelors would often stop by the cabin for a loaf of bread or a haircut. You had to bake bread every day. I think that's why today I find it almost second nature. But I was only baking white bread then. Isn't that awful? I didn't know anything about wheat germ."*

moved down in April. The cabin was built then, just one room about 12 by 14 feet."

They wanted to live on a remote homestead far from the outskirts of Anchorage, because they were going to farm, raise chickens, and sell the eggs and produce.

"Only we really hadn't thought it out too well," explains Marge, laughing. "You still can't do that 40 years later and make any money here."

But undaunted, that summer of 1948 they chopped down trees, pulled roots, and planted a garden of cabbage, potatoes, and carrots. During the next few years, war veterans began moving in and soon all the homestead lands surrounding them were claimed. There were few stipulations to settling the land under the old Homestead Act. Homesteaders could claim up to 160 acres if they built a habitable dwelling, lived in it for seven months out of the first three years, and cleared a certain percentage of the land. Once the surveying costs were paid, the land was theirs.

"The majority of homesteaders were single men," recounts Marge. "And I can say that for the first time in my life, I really missed the companionship of other women. The bachelors would often stop by the cabin for a loaf of bread or a haircut. You had to bake bread every day. I think that's why today I find it almost second nature. But I was

*The Mullen homestead cabin on Soldotna Creek, circa 1954. Left to right: Frank, Mary, young Frank, Marge, Peggy, and Eileen. (Mullen Collection)*

only baking white bread then. Isn't that awful? I didn't know anything about wheat germ."

Even when the women began to arrive, Marge was still fairly isolated from them. It was the men who traveled the road, borrowing equipment, going hunting, and exchanging news and ideas. In the classic sense, the women were tending the home fires and looking after the children. With the first money they could scrounge, they bought a battery-operated radio, a lifeline to news and people outside the homestead life. It wasn't an easy existence, but they were young and healthy and adventurous.

Tragically, that quickly changed.

In 1952, a polio epidemic swept through Alaska. With 1,000 chickens on order for spring laying season, three children all under the age of six squeezed into the tiny homestead cabin and a fourth child on the way, Frank went to bed complaining of a pain in his back, then his legs. Finally, he was immobile. Three days later he was evacuated out of Kenai by the Tenth Air Rescue,

*In 1952, a polio epidemic swept through Alaska. With 1,000 chickens on order for spring laying season, three children all under the age of six squeezed into the tiny homestead cabin and a fourth child on the way, Frank went to bed complaining of a pain in his back, then his legs. Finally, he was immobile.*

diagnosed as having poliomyelitis, and later sent to convalesce in a veteran's hospital in southern California.

He would never walk again. The doctors advised Marge to plan a different life. It was a cruel blow. She thought of moving somewhere else.

"With four children and one partner not able to work, I just didn't see how we could stay on the homestead." But they did. Frank returned in a wheelchair. Yet he could drive the tractor and with it plow the fields or go moose hunting and achieve a degree of mobility. "I was just glad he could get out of the house and get himself around," says Marge. "But I had to have 74 pairs of legs at least for all that we needed to do on the homestead."

With the help of her two brothers from Chicago, Marge added another room to the cabin and built the chicken house. There were also the daily chores—chopping wood, hauling water, cleaning the chicken house, collecting the eggs, pulling roots, planting, weeding, and harvesting, getting produce and eggs ready for sale, and taking care of four little children. To stave off cabin fever on those long dark winter nights, Marge would plan her dream house by the Kenai River in between cleaning lanterns, darning socks, patching frying pans, reading stories to the toddlers, and candling and boxing eggs for market.

The little cabin by the creek was only a temporary home until they could raise the money to build a more substantial one by the river. But like most homesteaders, the temporary cabin became a permanent one. It wasn't until 15 years later that they could afford to build another one or had the time to build. They were homesteaders who wanted to be farmers, so their efforts were primarily directed towards breaking the land.

Mary Mullen, the youngest, who is now 36 and has worked in politics, education, and counseling, has fond memories of growing up on the homestead. With dark brown hair and blue eyes, she is a classic Irish beauty.

"It wasn't until I was an adult

that I understood we were poor. Sociologists might call me deprived, but I knew I had had a rich childhood. Being the youngest, I didn't have to work as hard as everybody else. I spent a lot of time riding around on the tractor with my dad. Mom gave me a whistle to blow if we got stuck and needed help. Sometimes help came and sometimes it didn't. When it didn't, I quickly learned about chains and pulleys."

There was never much privacy. There were only two rooms. The three girls, Peggy, Eileen, and Mary, slept in bunk beds next to their parents in the little bedroom addition. The only boy in the family, Frank, slept on the couch in the main room of the cabin.

"But we experienced the woods, the fresh air, and we learned never to be afraid of people. The only thing I was sometimes scared about was getting between a cow moose and her calf on my way to school in the morning when it was dark," recalls Mary. "I don't know whether it was Mom or Dad or just growing up on a homestead, but there was always room for everybody in our lives. Sometimes after we moved into the new house by the river, there'd be so many people staying with us that two or three

*"It wasn't until I was an adult that I understood we were poor. Sociologists might call me deprived, but I knew I had had a rich childhood."*

—Mary Mullen

*Mary Mullen: "Sometimes there'd be so many people staying with us that two or three would be sleeping under the kitchen table." (Nan Elliot)*

*"We were always around a lot of really strong, courageous women. These homestead women did some incredible physical stuff, but they were still very traditional. They made sure when they got together that they gave themselves permanents just to keep up. You know, Leave-It-To-Beaver's mom would be doing the same thing in suburbia."*

—Peggy Mullen

*Peggy Mullen at Kachemak Bay, 1973: "To me, there's no room anymore for macho attitudes about the wilderness." (Nan Elliot)*

would be sleeping under the kitchen table and Mom always had a way of stretching a pot of stew.

"To me, mother is somewhat of a saint," she continues. "She's strong, selfless, always doing something for somebody else. She's a pretty cagey, imaginative woman. I'm surprised she's not completely loony-tunes trying to keep the homestead together after Dad got polio with four little kids. But she's the ultimate survivor. She's done what's necessary and gotten by, always with a happy attitude."

Each of Marge's children has grown in strong, independent ways. Yet most of the time they all live on the homestead or close by. "You have to have it in your head," says Marge "that your kids will go to the far-flung corners of the earth. My children all like to travel a lot, but so far they have chosen this place."

The oldest, Peggy, started a gourmet restaurant, "The Four Seasons," tucked among the birch trees on a corner of the homestead property. Later, she opened "Northcountry Fair," a shop of fancy and whimsical household gifts. She lives in a cabin on the river next to Marge. With curly blonde hair and a warm and easy manner, Peggy, as the oldest, shouldered a lot of the responsibility on the homestead. She remembers working in the fields 10 to 12 hours a day.

"Taking time off was rare. But we could always go swimming in the creek. Mom insisted on that. A lot of kids never learned to swim around here—the water's so cold—and many died in fishing accidents.

"We were always around a lot of really strong, courageous women. These homestead women did some incredible physical stuff, but they were still very traditional. They made sure when they got together that they gave themselves permanents just to keep up." Laughing, Peggy adds, "You know, Leave-It-To-Beaver's mom would be doing the same thing in suburbia."

"Margie loves being with her grandchildren now. There are six. It's probably a classic case of feeling she never had enough time for her own children. When you're hauling water and washing clothes on a scrub board with a raggle-taggle band of runny-nose kids behind you, you don't have a lot of time for a serious one-on-one with your children. So Marge always makes time for her grandchildren today."

Like her mother, Peggy is a champion of wild places.

"To me there's no room anymore for macho attitudes about the wilderness. I remember very clearly the moment I became an environmentalist. I was 10 years old. I was down at the creek at our bridge. This red-faced, overweight man was standing in the creek grabbing salmon out of the shallow water with his bare hands. He was showing off to two women. It seemed like such a cruel thing to do. The salmon were struggling to get upriver to spawn. There were fish swimming all around his feet. And he was wrestling with this huge king salmon. Of course, my heart went out to the fish. It needed to be in the water. We fished. But that's not how you took fish home to eat it. I guess it was the cruelty that impressed me. The two women were giggling. That's probably one of the reasons that has kept me from being a giggly woman today."

Eileen, the second oldest at age 41, is tall and blonde—a strong, handsome woman with a merry laugh. She is a fisherwoman. In the summer, she fishes salmon in Cook Inlet and in spring, she fishes halibut around Kodiak Island. She lives down the road in Kasilof with her two children.

"What I loved best about the homestead was having the forest at my doorstep. Mom never hovered. She never said, 'Watch

*"What I loved best about the homestead was having the forest at my doorstep. Mom never hovered. She never said, 'Watch out for the bears, watch out for the moose, and don't fall in the creek.' We weren't afraid to take off into the woods. She gave us confidence and a sense of adventure. We played with birds' nests and made tea out of bushes and climbed trees. We didn't have plastic toys."*

*—Eileen Mullen*

*Eileen Mullen: "Today, you often see women fishing. It's the adventure, the money, and the risk. It's always outdoors and it's never the same." (Nan Elliot)*

out for the bears, watch out for the moose, and don't fall in the creek.' We weren't afraid to take off into the woods. She gave us confidence and a sense of adventure. We played with birds' nests and made tea out of bushes and climbed trees. We didn't have plastic toys.

"I've never found any place I like better than Alaska. I'm sure development will happen. But I'll just get on my boat, sail to another wilderness and anchor up. Some place where the birds live and not the people. I love people. But I go to the wilderness to get replenished. Alaska means the freedom to do what I want.

"Today you often see women fishing. It's the adventure, the money, and the risk. It's always outdoors and it's never the same. When I started, I had to prove myself, prove myself, prove myself. There are still a few guys in awe of women fishermen. But we have all the intelligence and we're just as mechanical as men. We're not so much of an oddity anymore."

Skipper of the "Cloud 9," Frank, 39, is a salmon and halibut fisherman and also a local politician. He first built a log house for his family in the woods next to the old homestead garden. Then he moved them to a bigger home on the banks of the

Kenai River next to Marge. There's an engaging boyishness about Frank, reflected in his warmth and curiosity.

"In my life, the tide book means more to me than the calendar does. And I like that.

"I've done a lot of traveling on a lot of different continents. I've certainly enjoyed the traveling I've done. But it reinforces that this is my home. The drawbacks of winter darkness are far outweighed by the joys of summer light. The opportunities are here to make your own way through life without having to conform to 40-hour weeks and dress codes and social rules. You can set your own clock and operate by it.

When Frank remembers the happier times on the homestead, he says, "Gosh, we lived in a

*"The creek right next to our house was the main center of our daily life. It was full of salmon and trout. It was also where we got our water every day. In the winter, Marge would go down with an axe and chop a hole in the ice. My mom was carrying the water, literally and figuratively, for everybody."*

*—Frank Mullen*

minuscule place and many times we were very close. Some of my most vivid memories are when people from the outside world came to visit. In the dead of winter, there was the radio. It came with these huge batteries that Mom would order from the Sears catalogue. They would show up every fall and you hoped they would last until summer again or until the next barge could come in. We used to rush home after school, grab a piece of toast with currant jelly, and listen to some of those great serial radio stories of the '50s.

"Then we'd get occasional visitors. And boy, that was a big deal, you know, when somebody broke the spell and all of a sudden, there were new faces and new stories.

"The creek right next to our house was the main center of our daily life. It was full of salmon and trout. It was also where we got our water every day. In the winter, Marge would go down with an axe and chop a hole in the ice. My mom was carrying the water, literally and figuratively, for everybody. With a willow pole and a little fishing line I used to pull out beautiful rainbow trout, just effortlessly. I spent a lot of time falling into the creek and river and yanking stuff out for breakfast or supper. So I guess it was kind of natural I ended up a fisherman.

"A lot of living on the homestead was life and death stuff. I'm sure my mom had a lot of fear. But she overcame that out of the need to perform for her family. Marge has always been able to change with the times and with new ideas. She was anti-nuclear before most other people even knew how to spell it. And pro-environment."

"We used to have a diesel generator which provided our electricity during winter months. We shared the power with a few other families. Well, when it was our turn, Marge was the person who had to go over at seven every morning and start that son-of-a-bitch up. In January, it's 25 degrees below zero—you're walking half a mile down this narrow foot path, it's pitch black outside, and you've got moose as obstacles every 30 yards. I remember going over there with her, just tagging along as a little kid. And god, she'd be out there with her frozen hands—this little city girl from Chicago—cranking on this huge piece of equipment that was designed for a big, healthy male. It's hard for somebody who's never been there to understand. And that's just one of the things she was doing her whole life to get us by."

While others marvel at the history of Marge's life, the struggles to survive and make the homestead a reality, Marge does not really think she did anything remarkable. She is often quiet in a philosophical way and rarely talks about herself. But she loves to laugh and her laughter is a delight to hear. Her door is never locked and her house is like a pocket of warmth in the wilderness. With an invitation to stay freely extended, it is almost always filled with guests.

For her, the land is special. She has gone into debt paying the taxes before selling any part of the homestead. Located between the highway and the Kenai River, a fisherman's paradise, her land is a prized piece of real estate today, and the taxes are high.

"A lot of homesteaders came and they only saw the subdivid-

*The early morning baker at The Four Seasons, 1989.* (Nan Elliot)

*Peggy and Marge stand on the boardwalk to the gourmet Four Seasons restaurant, which they built in a grove of birch trees on a corner of the homestead property. (Nan Elliot)*

*"I love this country. When I first arrived, I never knew that land could inspire such fierce tenacity. This is nature in its force and you have to be in tune with it."*

*—Marge Mullen*

ing possibilities," says Marge. "My view was not whether the land could make me money except through agriculture. I love this country. When I first arrived, I never knew that land could inspire such fierce tenacity. This is nature in its force and you have to be in tune with it."

But her bond to Alaska goes far beyond the land. She always seems to have a cause. No venture is too small if it will make

life just a little bit better, whether it's lobbying her congressman to get a ramp for wheelchairs included in the blueprints of the new Soldotna post office, picking broken glass out of the gravel by the lake where little children go swimming in the summer, organizing a garbage pick-up day in town, or clearing wilderness trails. She always deflects any modicum of praise. Rather she says, "You see this neighborhood develop and you want to see it guided in a useful, and maybe a beautiful, way. Yet that hardly seems possible sometimes in a developing country, because how things look doesn't seem to be anybody's prime concern."

Early every morning, Marge is at The Four Seasons restaurant baking bread, doing what she's been doing for the last 30 years, except this time it's with whole wheat flour and for paying customers. Only since the restaurant opened in 1977 has Marge had the money to take a vacation.

But she once remarked, "Life's small moments are much more special than trying for great wealth."

A moment of sanctuary underneath a bush near the river bank, the wind upon her cheeks, the exhilaration of the sunrise, peeling logs, or even weeding the garden, these are still her favorite times.

# 8

# The Great Ocean Spirit

*Where the mountains plunge to the sea, the Great Ocean Spirit Gonaqadet welcomed Raven to a rich feast. Once finished, the kindly spirit donned his exquisite dancing robe. Drums echoed the pounding waves as Gonaqadet swung his body rhythmically to the music. In the ghostly light of the fire, he became a wolf . . . a bear . . . an eagle. Raven's heart beat wildly. When the dance was done, the generous spirit offered Raven his beautiful dancing blanket. Raven flew away and in time offered his gift to women so they might unravel the mysteries of the blanket and weave it again. It was in this way that the women brought great glory to the Indian people of the coast.*

*—Tlingit Story*

*Rosita Worl: "I like to be outside on the beach. I like to make the call of the Raven. But sometimes, I just like to fly. I am an Eagle." (Rob Stapleton)*

Isolated from the interior by dark, forbidding mountains, the Indians of the North Pacific settled this long, narrow strip of coastline that one day would be called Alaska. They built their villages in sheltered coves or along riverbanks and forged remarkable civilizations. The Haida were great carvers. The Tsimshian were known as "people of many riches." But it was the Tlingits who dominated this far northern coast. They were fierce warriors.

Today, the modern-day descendants of these early Indian peoples of southeast Alaska may often be found behind steel and glass structures wielding power, publishing stories, or perhaps even teaching the ancient arts with a new flair. But their lives are still governed by some memory of the old ways—the call of the Eagle or the Raven, the pounding of the drums, the gathering of spruce roots and berries, the ebb and flow of the ocean.

The late Roger Lang was a Tsimshian and a Tlingit. First he worked as a fisherman and a ferry boat captain. In later years, he spent much of his life in a three-piece suit sitting behind a corporate desk as president of the most powerful political and educational Native organizations in Alaska.

"Whether you are Indian, Aleut, or Eskimo, if you can get to the ocean, you get to the ocean. That's living," Roger once said. "The goal of any Native leader is to manage change. That's all you can do, for change is inevitable.

You cannot stop it. People allow me to be a leader. It's not any great assumption on my part of worthiness. It's just circumstance. My real ultimate dream is to go back to the ocean."

Rosita Worl is Tlingit. Harvard-educated, she is a former professor of anthropology and publisher of Alaska's only Native magazine.

"Native people don't view themselves apart from the land and water and sky. They don't make the separations between the spirits of animals and spirits of people. I like to be outside on the beach. I like to make the call of the Raven. But sometimes, I just like to fly. I am an Eagle. I belong to the Thunderbird Clan on the Eagle side. When the Thunderbird passes, I also have his spirit. I don't know if I could point to a bird and say that that is a Thunderbird. But I can tell you when he is here. That is when you see lightning. Lightning is the blinking of the Thunderbird's eye and thunder is the flapping of its wings."

Delores Churchill is Haida. Growing up in a little village in the Queen Charlotte Islands, she collected sea gull eggs to eat in the spring and in the summer helped to harvest and dry fish. She was good at math, but never bothered to learn English, sure

*The modern-day descendants of these early Indian peoples of southeast Alaska may often be found behind steel and glass structures wielding power, publishing stories, or perhaps even teaching the ancient arts with a new flair. But their lives are still governed by some memory of the old ways—the call of the Eagle or the Raven, the pounding of the drums, the gathering of spruce roots and berries, the ebb and flow of the ocean.*

*The late Roger Lang was Tsimshian and Tlingit. A fisherman and ferry boat captain, he was also president of the most powerful political and educational Native organizations in Alaska.* (Anchorage Times)

anthropologist. It said that basketry had a greater influence on people's lives than the invention of the wheel. When people learned to weave baskets, they could make containers for food; they could make clothing instead of wearing furs and animal skins; they could make thatched roofs. All of a sudden it hit me. Everyone started from a basketry background. It wasn't mine. It didn't belong to me as an Indian. It actually belongs to everyone. We all have a common origin."

\*     \*     \*

she would never need it. She spoke only Haida. She laughs about that today. English has become an essential. For today, she travels all over the world teaching the ancient art of basketry.

"The Tlingits didn't know how to carve totem poles. They learned from the Haida. And it was the Tsimshian who first did the Raven weave. We all learn from each other. Weaving ties us to our ancestors, to past generations.

"I used to be very selfish with basketry. It should only be done by Indian people, I thought. Then in Boston I read an article by an

Today, Native peoples in Alaska live in a mixture of subsistence and cash economies, village and urban life. By the year 2000, subsistence may not be a reality, said Roger Lang. That was the issue of the 1970s. In the 1980s and into the '90s, the issue is land.

Once Natives receive full title to their land, as directed under the Alaska Native Land Claims Settlement Act of 1971, Eskimo, Aleut, and Indian people collectively will become the third largest landlord in Alaska next to the state and federal governments, and they will be the largest private landholder.

A few years ago, as Roger Lang looked to the future of

Native people in Alaska, he stressed two areas of critical importance.

"We must hold on to our lands. But the one thing we cannot lose is our individual Native identity. I'm not Native. There's no identity to being Native. I am a Tsimshian and a Tlingit."

Born in the village of Metlakatla on an island in southeast Alaska, Roger grew up under the powerful influences of his two grandmothers. Although one grandfather was Norwegian and the other a Tlingit, both his grandmothers were Tsimshian Indians who had emigrated from Canada to Annette Island in southern Alaska.

"One died when I was eight, the other when I was 16. But I can still close my eyes and see them now," he said, leaning back in his chair, hands behind his head.

"They influence me . . . even today. My grandmothers gave me the strength to take risks—to stick my neck out. I'm still doing that.

"It's true of almost any southeastern culture—Tsimshian, Tlingit, and Haida—the women are power. In lineage, you are everything your mother and grandmother are and nothing that your father is. It's a very matriarchal society. The women tend to rule, but never out front. They are strong like the ocean—they can scare you to death, but they can make you so happy. They can provide you with a living or give you the strength to live.

"When you are Tsimshian, you know who you are and where you come from. When my son was born, my mother came to see him. She took him in her arms and in Tsimshian told him who he was, what the world was like, and why he was here. That's very important. Women start very early doing that. If you know these two things it really doesn't matter what people do to you or say about you. You know what you are. Plus, it always gives me what I call the reversion clause. If I don't like what I am here, I can always go back to being Native in nothing flat. It's interesting to look at the vacation patterns of my friends who are Native also. They do a lot of vacationing, but when they're serious, they always go home."

Roger was part of the last generation of Tsimshians and Tlingits to get their education primarily from listening to the stories of their grandparents and the elders of the community.

"What really interests me is that they call our history 'myth and lore' and they call yours

*"It's true of almost any southeastern culture—Tsimshian, Tlingit, and Haida—the women are power. It's a very matriarchal society. Women tend to rule, but never out front. They are strong like the ocean—they can scare you to death, but they can make you so happy."*

*—Roger Lang*

*Roger Lang.* (Anchorage Times)

'history.' And you're debating the creation of man, whether to teach Adam's rib or evolution in the schools, but hell, neither is true. Man came from a series of things . . . red cedar, rocks, and flowers." Roger laughed with a certain mischievous delight. "It's as good a story as yours is, for Christ's sake," he added, grinning.

\*　　\*　　\*

The power of the ocean and the strength of their women is an echo that reverberates throughout Tsimshian, Haida, and Tlingit cultures.

"Tlingit philosophers talk of waves of change," says Rosita Worl. "The power of the ocean can be seen in the metaphors we use. Like the river flowing to the sea, that's the way Tlingits are. We continue to flow into the ocean. We have always been fishermen. That's Tlingit life and Tlingit culture.

"I belong here. I can feel my ancestors paddling their cedar canoes up Lynn Canal. It's a wonderful feeling to know that you and your people have been here for thousands and thousands of years."

Born in a little cabin on the beach in Petersburg, Rosita had little formal education. Whatever she learned in school as a child was only a sprinkling compared to the training she received from her mother, a union organizer in the salmon canneries of southeast Alaska. Rosita worked in the canneries before the enforcement of child labor laws and she kept the minutes of those covert meetings to rally support for a union which would guarantee rights to Native workers in the face of a powerful Alaska salmon industry.

Rosita was not raised in the traditional role of a Tlingit

woman. She was too rambunctious. Her mother allowed her to go fishing with her uncle, an apprenticeship usually reserved for the young men in the family.

"I was part of the problem as identified by white society—the Indian problem. They always talked about it. We weren't educated. We weren't employed. We weren't good steady workers. As soon as salmon cannery season came, I don't care what job I was doing, I'd take off and go work in the cannery. Just so I could do all the things I grew up doing and enjoyed doing, like drying fish, picking berries, and going clamming.

"And maybe I drank a little too much. I was every bit of that Indian problem. But I tell you, I sure enjoyed myself. I laughed a lot and I felt good."

Today, Rosita has a doctorate degree from Harvard University. Formerly a professor of anthropology at the University of Alaska, she started and became the publisher of *Alaska Native Magazine*. Recently, she also served as special assistant to the governor of Alaska for Native and rural affairs.

"Very definitely I have changed. It happened when I became educated. My mother died when I was 26. It was a very significant moment in my life. I was selected to take her place and I received in a very old traditional ceremony her 'koogeina,' a banner with the words 'Alaska Native Sisterhood.'"

That ceremony was the passage of a heritage, strength, and beliefs from mother to daughter.

"I went on a month's retreat," she remembers. "And I really thought about the contributions my mother had made to Tlingit society. And here I was rolling along my merry way labeled as 'the Indian problem.' I looked at what was really going on. I saw our relationship to white people as very oppressed. We worked in the canneries alongside people who were getting twice as much pay. Our children were dropping out of school. Only 30 Tlingits were in college with a dropout rate of 60 percent. When I saw that some of the members of my own family were alcoholics, that's when it really hit me.

"'What has happened?' I thought. 'We were really proud, strong people once.' When I realized this, I became politically active. I worked to recruit Tlingit students for college. I finally enrolled myself.

"College was such a fantastic experience," Rosita remembers. "I used to read all the time. It took me four times as long as anyone

*Rosita Worl.* (Anchorage Daily News)

*"I was part of the problem as identified by white society—the Indian problem. They always talked about it. We weren't educated. We weren't employed. We weren't good steady workers. As soon as salmon cannery season came, I don't care what job I was doing, I'd take off and go work in the cannery. Just so I could do all the things I grew up doing and enjoyed doing, like drying fish, picking berries, and going clamming."*

*—Rosita Worl*

else to finish books. But it was like a curtain opening up for me. I was seeing a whole different world. All of a sudden, I graduated. And I hadn't even begun to learn what I wanted to yet." So she went on for her doctorate.

"I went to school not to become educated for myself, but educated to do a task for Native people. That's the kind of socialization we have—to think not only of yourself, but also for the group. If Tlingit people could teach other people special things about the world, I would teach people about the value of thinking of yourself as part of a group and being concerned for the survival of the group. One thing that really bothers me is to see even Native people becoming increasingly dependent on institutions to take care of needs, to take care of the family, to take care of our neighbors.

"I have changed a lot in the last 20 years. I think I'm a successful person because I know who I am as a Tlingit. But I am also very comfortable on the board of directors for the Harvard Club or as a professor at the university. I have learned how to fit into both worlds, both Tlingit and white. They are two different worlds that overlap. I am a little of both. But I can go both ways. A lot of Native people have not made that distinction yet."

\*　　　\*　　　\*

As women unraveled the mysteries of the Great Spirit's dancing robe, they wove it again with threads of copper, mountain goat hair, and yellow cedar. The greatest weavers lived in the Chilkat Mountains of southeast Alaska. The dancing robe became known as the Chilkat blanket and it was a prized possession.

In the old days, in the darkness of winter, people gathered in their houses of cedar. It was a time for weaving, carving, and telling stories. It was also a time for potlatches—elaborate celebrations of feasting, gambling, and dancing—in honor of the dead or to glorify the living. To impress the assembled with his wealth, a chief might sacrifice several slaves, or, perhaps in an even more extravagant moment, cut his cherished dancing blanket into strips, giving them as gifts to his guests.

Chilkat weaving today is a treasured art. Perhaps only a dozen women know its secrets. Delores Churchill is one of them. Her first creation was a dancing apron. It is an eagle. Delores belongs to the Eagle Beaver Frog Clan. In stylized patterns, one can see on the finely woven apron the head of the eagle, the mouth, the claws, the stomach, and the tail feathers. Hanging from the bottom, softly rattling as the dancer sways to the music, are deer hide thongs tied with puffin beaks and deer claws.

"Mostly witch doctors used the dancing apron," says Delores. "The blanket, apron, and leggings—they're very ceremonial. My apron has been in lots of ceremonies. I let other people wear it. It likes to dance." Her eyes shine brightly. Underneath her curly gray hair, Delores has a wonderful childlike exuberance about the world.

"Cut-up pieces of a Chilkat blanket are more valuable than the whole blanket itself because they are given at a potlatch.

"But, as the weaver," she smiles shyly, "if someone cut up my blanket, I would cry."

There are several chiefs in Delores' family. "In white ways, I would be a princess," she says. "But it isn't that way in Indian ways. The person who is the chief is honored. You are not recognized in the village unless you do something special."

From her village in the Queen Charlotte Islands, Delores moved with her family first to Prince Rupert in Canada and at the age of 16, to Ketchikan, Alaska. Her

*Ketchikan at the turn of the century. (Case & Draper Photographers, Alaska Historical Library)*

mother, Selina Peratrovich, was a well-known and highly respected basket weaver and teacher. In the spring they would go into the forest and collect spruce roots and red cedar for their basket-making.

"My mother always thanked the tree and said she would be back. And she always talked to bears when we were out berry picking. She'd say, 'I'm a woman. I'm not out here to hurt you. I'm just here to pick berries as you are picking berries.' She always spoke to them. It was common courtesy," remembers Delores.

"When I first started weaving Chilkat, my mother was really upset, because she said Haidas didn't do that. It was Tlingit. But

*Delores Churchill, basketry teacher, wearing her Chilkat dancing apron.*
(Nan Elliot)

*"Mostly witch doctors used the dancing apron. The blanket, apron, and leggings—they're very ceremonial. My apron has been in lots of ceremonies. I let other people wear it. It likes to dance."*

—Delores Churchill

the way the story goes, the Tsimshians were the first to do this Chilkat weaving. And then it went up the coast and the Tlingit people started it—the Cape Fox people and the Tongass tribes—and then it went all the way up the coast to the people of Haines and Yakutat. So I'm sure the Haidas would have started doing it too, because the totem poles originated with the Haidas and moved up and down the coast."

Delores is a basketry teacher. But she wanted to learn Chilkat weaving so badly she went to the

weaving teacher and said, "I can't eat. I can't sleep. I'm acting like I'm in love. You have to take me in your class."

Her second apron is the Diving Whale.

"I'm having a really hard time letting this one go. I love it so much. The forms are perfect. I have avoided putting in the eyes yet. As soon as the eyes are in, it takes on a personality of its own and you cannot look at those eyes for long. You are driven to finish.

"It wants to dance."

# 9

# King Pin

**I**f death and sex sell, this little puppy is really gonna take off," claimed the seemingly mild-mannered fellow with silver hair and tweed-jacket respectability.

Beware.

High up on Chicken Ridge, in the middle of the capital city of Juneau, sits a stately blue and white residence. Sometimes, it is mistaken by tourists for the British Consulate or the Russian Embassy. Depending upon the whimsy of its occupant, it is occasionally known as "The Unspeakable Acts Research Center: Moth-to-Flame Division."

Formerly, it was "Snappy Graphics." That's when Bill Spear was peddling his humor from bar to bar.

Now he sells his art from Prudhoe Bay, Alaska, to the Guggenheim Museum in New York City. In a moment of seriousness, he renamed his studio home to the more exalted elevation of "Wm Spear Design." Still, if you are invited to spend a night in the guest room, you will find

*Artist Bill Spear hoists the Jolly Roger over Juneau. His first enamel pin creation, which he called "Death and Sex," took off like a rocket.*
(Joel Bennett)

*Bill climbs through the trap door onto his roof (a.k.a. "Bill's Rain Forest Tanning Salon"), lowers the Union Jack or the People's Republic of China or whatever other inflammatory flag he is currently flying, and runs up the pirate skull and crossbones of the Jolly Roger instead. When they passed a law to shorten bar hours in Juneau, Bill was back on the roof. "They should punish the people who **drive** you to drink—**not** the people who drink," he declared.*

your bed turned down, a chocolate on the pillow, dancing skeletons in top hats on the wall, and a bottle of shampoo on the bedside table reading: "Snappy Motel and Lounge. Ask for Bill."

From his perch on the ridge, the artist-in-residence has a commanding view of the icy waters of Gastineau Channel, the flight of eagles in courtship, and the shenanigans of Alaska politicians who congregate every January to June just down the hill in the State Capitol Building.

And when Bill is incensed—which he often is—by some infuriating action of the Alaska Legislature, everybody in Juneau knows it.

Up goes the Jolly Roger.

Bill climbs through the trap door onto his roof (a.k.a. "Bill's Rain Forest Tanning Salon"), lowers the Union Jack or the People's Republic of China or whatever other inflammatory flag he is currently flying, and runs up the pirate skull and crossbones of the Jolly Roger instead. When they passed a law to shorten bar hours in Juneau, Bill was back on the roof.

"They should punish the people who *drive* you to drink—*not* the people who drink," he declared.

Formerly, this pirate flag-waver was a lawyer, deputy commissioner of labor, and chairman of the board of the largest venture capital bank in the world.

But at age 39, all the springs

*From his studio high up on Chicken Ridge, Bill Spear has a commanding view of Mt. Jumbo, the town of Juneau, and the icy waters of Gastineau Channel. It is here in the "Unspeakable Acts Research Center" that he brandishes his formidable wit and humor.* (Joel Bennett)

started popping loose. He threw his cards up in the air and took a year's sabbatical roaring around Italy on his motorcycle. The result? The little boy who used to draw 20-foot-long underwater murals on the blackboard back in Nebraska before the kindergarten teacher arrived for school is finally doing what he really loves. Making art. Funny art, renegade art, popular art.

Today, Bill Spear is a cartoonist, pin designer, and entrepreneur. (He has always been a

master raconteur and closet blues singer.)

On his father's side, Spear comes from a long line of Scottish entrepreneurs who settled in the Midwest—shoe merchants, general merchandisers, and one artful horse handler who rode with Buffalo Bill Cody's Wild West Show. His mother was adopted. So half of Bill's background is, as he says, "blacked out."

"Sometimes when I have this unaccountable behavior, I think,

THE MANY FACES OF BILL SPEAR. Cruising the streets of Juneau. *(Joel Bennett)*

Parading in his annual skunk cabbage costume, which he describes as "unwearable art." *(Nan Elliot)*

Delivering seasonal blessings from the Juneau ice field. *(Spear Collection)*

*Bill Spear sincerely wants to be a good guy. But it's a struggle. A highly-charged, profit-oriented, entrepreneurial spirit beats warmly in Bill's heart.*

'God, my mother could have been the daughter of a famous painter, or a trapeze artist, or a stunt pilot . . . god knows what! Probably I'm a direct descendant of John Quincy Adams!'" says Bill with a laugh. "For my mother, it's horrible not to know any of her past. But for me, it's kind of intriguing to have some of it a mystery."

"Wm Spear Design" is only six years old. Yet from coast to coast, Bill is quickly achieving notoriety and fame.

Don't be deceived by first im-pressions. He will fool you. He looks like a dapper, east coast preppie. He's really a half-crazed artist who fantasizes about beautiful women and draws classic symbols of death.

He's a political conservative in favor of development. But he has the heart of a rabid conservationist. Nothing makes him madder than somebody clear-cutting trees in the forest.

He has a lot of the traditional values like loyalty, propriety, keeping promises, and adhering to the highest standard of qual-

*"The skull to me is not a symbol of death. It is a symbol of life. It is the seat of the thing which makes human beings unique, the brain. Traditionally, a 'memento mori' was painted into a lot of Renaissance art. It was a reminder of death. It was not meant to be depressing, rather to inspire people to live life better."*

ity. Yet he cultivates the image of the reckless, heartless playboy with a kind of French commando flair. He adores cranking up "his little puppy," a 25-year-old Jaguar antique sports car he calls "Slick," and going as fast as he can without getting arrested.

Bill Spear sincerely wants to be a good guy. But it's a struggle. A highly-charged, profit-oriented, entrepreneurial spirit beats warmly in Bill's heart.

He wants his art—his finely enameled pins—to be retailed like Cartier jewelry in a little box on a velvet cushion, where, if you pay $1,000, you get to keep the pillow. On the other hand, he wants to be the billboard painter, creating art that everyone can share.

No matter what the seeming contradictions, for today at least, he is the billboard painter, selling his art inch by inch . . . and getting rich.

"Death and Sex," his first enamel pin, took off like a rocket.

He had just read a book in which the author claimed that advertisers camouflage powerful images of sex into their message to get the viewer to buy their products. Half jokingly, he drew the word "SEX" into the design, a Jolly Roger with a red heart floating on a black background.

The shape of the skull is an "s," the teeth form an "e," and the bones are an "x." There it was, in black and white, SEX and death. Throw in the red heart and it was sometimes known as "Love is Poison."

This was the first in a series of "bad boy pins," as Bill calls them.

It was quickly followed by "RIDE HARD, DIE FREE," a white skull on black enamel with a pirate's bandana wrapped around its cranium. This pin has topped the charts not only with bikers and barflies, but with Russian aviators and visiting Chinese diplomats. A number-one favorite, it has many variations. The *Anchorage Daily News* asked for a company pin: "WRITE HARD, DIE FREE," which features the skull in front of a computer monitor. When the Alaska economy began to dive in the mid-1980s and generously-paid state bureaucrats were resisting any salary cuts, Bill came out with another skull pin wearing a green visor: "FREE RIDES DIE HARD."

Pirates, skulls, and bones figure prominently in Bill's artistic fantasies. Lizards and snakes run a close second. Throughout Snappy Motel there are real-life bones and skulls; dancing plastic skeletons; skull rings with ruby eyes; paper cutouts of skeletons in top hats or at tea parties; and cartoons of black-caped skull executioners.

Bill calls all his macabre little toys "dime store bad things."

In five years, he has created hundreds of enamel pins (only be sure to call them "jewelry" when you talk to Bill). Among them are dozens of skulls—sinking skulls, exploding skulls, flaming skulls, flying skulls, skulls in hats, skulls and bones, skulls and skeletons, and skulls with wild messages.

For many, these are images from the darker side of life.

But the artist—with his choir-boy pink cheeks and blue eyes—disagrees. "The skull to me is not a symbol of death. It is a symbol of life. It is the seat of the thing which makes human beings unique, the brain. Traditionally, a 'memento mori' was painted into a lot of Renaissance art. It was a reminder of death. It was not meant to be depressing, rather to inspire people to live life better. That's what "Ride Hard Die Free" means. People write it off as a biker's pin. But, if you don't ride hard and you sit around and vegetate, essentially you're going to die a captive. To me, that's not a death notion. It's a life notion."

Among his brilliant-colored array of pins, Bill has art pins, science pins, fish pins, bird pins, animal pins, flag pins, and humorous pins. Each one has his home phone number on the back. So as they say, "you can reach out and touch him." Pretty soon though, he's going to change the number if his fans in different time zones keep reaching out in the middle of the night, demanding "What the hell does *this* pin mean?"

His 500 clients around the country include the Smithsonian, National Geographic, New York Historical Society, Guggenheim Museum, Monterey Bay Aquarium, Willow Trading Post, and Stampa Barbara. Big and little, rich and poor, they're all wearing "Bill Spear Pins."

Some of his most popular ones in Alaska are the skulls, fish, birds, and message pins. For a state where the alcohol consumption is the highest per capita in the country, "The Night My Goddamned Drink Caught on Fire" is a bestseller. In golds, reds, blues, and blacks, it shows an ice-filled drink tipped on one edge with flames shooting out of it.

"A visual image is not reducible to words," says the artist. "You can see people glance at a pin for a nano-second and then demand to know what it means.

*He reworked the current flag of Alaska—the Big Dipper and the North Star. Instead of a background of blue, which it is today, he chose international socialist red. He calls it "The People's Republic of Alaska."*

*Spear sports an array of his "bad boy" pins—only be sure to call them "jewelry" when you talk to Bill.* (Joel Bennett)

Some people get really angry like you're trying to pull something over on them or make fool of them. Like the drink on fire. I don't know what it means. The basis is some kind of alcoholic frustration with fire and ice imagery. The glass is upset. Little sparks fly out. It's real active and aggressive, yet with a sense of humor. It's a nice nighttime pin. It's black and gold and glitters."

What would the flag look like if Russia had not sold Alaska to the United States? Bill has a pin.

He reworked the current flag of Alaska—the Big Dipper and the North Star. Instead of a background of blue, which it is today, he chose international socialist red. He calls it "The People's Republic of Alaska."

For those who don't like Bill Spear pins or are too embarrassed to wear one, he's got an answer—the camo pin—all in greens and browns of military camouflage.

"Here's a pin you can wear and remain undetected," he says.

For those who are more flamboyant, Spear loves to encourage wearing more than one pin. Pins can be combined as "visual puns," he says. For example, you

can wear the Madonna and the Holstein to say "Holy Cow!" Or you can cross two of the medical science pins—epidermal and brain—to get "skinhead." A pink elephant pinned next to the martini glass is a warning that if you drink too much you may start seeing these rosy behemoths.

At the beginning of the whole pin adventure, even though he likes to shake things up and roll the dice, Bill was typically nervous. "At first, I was selling at the bars. Here I am, the former chairman of the board of the Alaska Renewable Resources Corporation, probably the largest venture capital bank in the world, and I'm selling little jewelry in plastic bags out of my pocket for three to five dollars. I felt real queasy in that situation.

"For a long time, I had no status. It was like going from hero to zero," he says, still nervous today even though he's a raging success.

"This pin thing—I couldn't have done it in a lot of other places. The social pressure would have been too strong for me to stay being an attorney. I would have gone on being kind of unhappy.

"But people in Alaska are very encouraging to change. In a sense, they root for you. People bought my pins and had confidence when I didn't that this was really an acceptable thing to do. I feel I've kept up my end of it by being kind of successful, making a little splash outside the state, which I think Alaskans like. They're very proud when one of their number does something worthwhile outside their arena.

"I like Alaska for the personal freedom it allows. The place has been good for me. I've done things here that wouldn't have occurred to me if I'd stayed in Nebraska. In the 1950s, in Nebraska, being an artist was not something you encouraged your kid to do," says Bill, who describes himself then as a loud and obnoxious kid with an uneventful childhood.

"In the Midwest, the whole town participates in your upbringing. Everyone is a spy. There are only two ways to make it. You either embrace the system or you get out." Spear got out. He graduated from Georgetown University's School of Foreign Service and tended bar at Clyde's in Washington, D.C.

"I made good money as a bartender. The busboy then now owns half of Clyde's and is a multi-millionaire. I should have stayed," he adds, not entirely as a joke.

But the dutiful son, he went back to Nebraska to attend law school. He got married his senior year and had two children, now teenagers. He says the years he was married were good years. Yet, as one of his cartoons about life says, "Marital problems? Yep. You bet." And the drawing shows a woman marching out the door, wearing (as the arrow and notation read) what else but "sensible shoes."

Before that all happened, however, Bill and his wife were lured up to Alaska by a job in the attorney general's office and lived in the big house on Chicken Ridge, so named because the early Juneau gold miners couldn't spell "ptarmigan," the fat little birds they were shooting and eating. Or so the story goes.

"I always like the rush of being on a new adventure and being with good people. We had a kind of Alamo mentality—the small forces of good against the huge forces of evil. That's part of the reason why this town has the character it does. There are very few state capitals that have the same kind of issues this one does—oil money being the main one. I mean, there's a lot of meat on the table. Raw meat. That's pretty heady stuff."

"But there are other reasons

*An old, weathered prospector told newcomer Billy Spear one rainy evening in a dark bar in Juneau, "You know, if you stay up here long enough, sometime you'll be sitting somewhere and you'll look up. And there will be a scene so emotionally moving and so powerful that wherever you go in the world, that scene will always appear to you and draw you back to the north."*

why Alaska is such a unique place," says Bill. "When I first came up, everything was so new and exciting.

"I had this fantasy about sailing around the world like everyone does. In most places, it would be written off as just that—fantasy. I had a secretary who was a wonderful woman. There was something in her eyes. She was always in a good humor. She'd lived in the Bush for years and years. But then her husband had a heart attack. So they came to town.

"At coffee breaks, I'd fantasize, and she kept nodding and grinning and saying, 'Yeah, that'd be great to do that . . . Yeah, well, we sure liked it.'

"And I said, 'What?'

"'Oh, yeah, we sailed around the world. My husband built the boat. Kids went too.'

"I knew they didn't have much money. 'How'd you learn to navigate?' I asked.

"'Well, we were at the Salvation Army and found a bunch of these old navigational charts from the 1940s. So we just got those and sailed straight south.'

"Can you believe it? No lessons. Nothing. That to me really captures the promise of Alaska. It holds out the real possibility. You can't say, 'Oh, I could never do that.' Because you could. And there'd be people around who'd have done it and would help you. You pay for it. After an experience like that, you become a different person—someone who is not really a marketable member of the IBM sales staff. You've got a whole collection of those positive, adventurous people up here.

"All Alaskans—true Alaskans—have a great love for the land. When you take the name of a place and use it to describe yourself, it seems to me the test is your love for that physical location."

One day, his first year in Juneau, Bill was sitting in a bar next to an old prospector, a classic looking guy with rugged, weathered features.

The old-timer said to Bill, "You know, if you stay up here

long enough, sometime you'll be sitting somewhere and you'll look up. And there will be a scene so emotionally moving and so powerful that wherever you go in the world, that scene will always appear to you and draw you back to the north."

Well, thought Bill, that was a nice sentiment, but he didn't pay much attention until the first time he went hunting. It was December 1.

"The whole expedition was foolhardy," he grins. There he was in the middle of winter deep into Tracy Arm, a spectacular, cliff-lined, glacial fjord in the wilderness south of Juneau.

"A friend with zero experience took us out in this ancient boat he had just bought. We thought we were going goat hunting. There was a bunch of us. I was completely ill-prepared. I had borrowed a rifle. My friend Joel was with me, but then we split up. This huge deer appeared. I realized finally we were hunting deer, not goats. But I didn't know how to hunt, where to shoot, or how to dress them.

"All of a sudden, this majestic animal was standing before me and I was so excited.

"Anyway, I shot the damn thing and then was so worked up and excited about it, both good and bad. Here I—who had

*"Anyway, I shot the damn thing and then was so worked up and excited about it, both good and bad. Here I—who had been against hunting—had reduced this wonderful living creature to an inanimate object. I felt horrible."*

been against hunting—had reduced this wonderful living creature to an inanimate object. I felt horrible. But I rationalized those feelings by convincing myself that someone somewhere had to kill animals for me to eat, unless I was a vegetarian, which I was not. Fortunately, Joel heard the shot and came to help me gut and clean it.

"Tracy Arm is steep cliffs on both sides. There's only a few places you can get back down to the water. December is when you have pale, beautiful light. The fjord was chuck full of huge icebergs from the glacier.

"We dragged the deer down to what would have been a beach, if there were a beach. Then we waited for the boat. After sitting there a while, I looked up and here was this gigantic iceberg—brilliant ice blue. The sky was shimmering gold with that rosy, cold, cold light you have in winter. The trees were dark and majestic.

*"I always like the rush of being on a new adventure and being with good people," says Bill, whose life philosophy is "Don't die wondering."* (Joel Bennett)

The water was a deep ice blue-green. I can see it in my head right now. Just like the old man said. I'm sure it was all wrapped up, as this guy in the bar knew, with the whole emotional experience, the trauma and excitement, of killing the deer. I'll never forget it."

Bill is thoughtful for a moment.

"You know, I much prefer being in the field, rather than home in the fort. You've got to have being home in the fort to rest up. But I like the expeditions. I like to be out there, whether it's mental or physical.

"The pin business is still thrilling to me. Always changing. One day, my pins will be in the Louvre," he declares, only half joking. "Well, maybe only for sale in the gift shop," he adds with a sly laugh.

"You see, an artist is always looking for immortality. Like the salmon who lays 4,000 eggs to ensure the species' survival, this is my biological strategy. The work itself is durable. And there are thousands of them. A few will undoubtedly survive the centuries and end up in the Louvre as a rare, historic piece of art.

"And think of it, maybe they'll still be calling my number."

# 10

# "Give 'Em Hale!"

*B*orn in a small New England setting at the beginning of the roaring twenties, our hero seemed to have all the cards stacked against him—wealth, connections, a solid family, a good classical education, social standing—in short, all the things that ruin most people and cause them to become boring, middle-class fools who contribute nothing to the world and usually drive the rest of us to drink . . .

This portrait of Commander John Hale, taken in 1945, hangs in the Naval Academy Athletic Hall of Fame. (U.S. Navy photographer)

So begins the cartoon-illustrated story entitled *Another John Hale Adventure: He's Going Like Sixty,* presented by cartoonist Billy Spear to John Hale upon the occasion of Hale's 60th birthday in 1982.

The first cartoon box under the title shows the speedometer of a car rapidly accelerating to 60 miles per hour. Hale, in the driver's seat, has lifted his hands gleefully from the wheel as the car goes careening down the road and exclaims to his passenger: "Hey Jeff, look! No hands!"

Jeff Macktaz (alias "Mr. Rock and Roll"), a young rock concert promoter and friend well familiar with life in the fast lane, is a cowering unseen mass on the floor of the car. A word bubble from his direction says: "Jesus, John, slow down a little, will ya . . .?!"

Once met, John Hale is not forgotten.

He has twice the energy of anyone half his age and his voice is the loudest in the room. He's gruff, aggressive, and brilliant with a knack for making things happen.

First and foremost, he loves people and is devoted to making his friends happy, often in unorthodox ways. He'll rant and rave and swear at them one moment and the next be hugging and kissing them. He'll argue with them, fight with them, give them his money, get them a job, build them a house, buy them land, write and sing them a song, and if they're shy, propose marriage for them to someone they know—or someone they don't know—in the middle of a bar or every hour on the hour over the air waves at his wilderness radio station KABN (pronounced "cabin") at "Radio Free Big Lake, Alaska."

Because of his naval background and his impressive ath-

*He has twice the energy of anyone half his age and his voice is the loudest in the room. He's gruff, aggressive, and brilliant with a knack for making things happen.*

letic achievements—All-American athlete, captain of the 1945 Naval Academy wrestling team, 1952 Olympic finalist, Naval Academy Athletic Hall of Fame—John Hale is known to many in Alaska simply as "The Commander."

A large, rowdy friend, "Big Bad Billy McConkey," who has run more than 40 successful political campaigns across the country, takes a long breath of wind before describing John Hale.

"Strangers who meet him for the first time are put off, because he's so loud and abrupt and because it never seems to stop. The guy keeps wanting to say, 'Yea, but . . .' and he never gets a chance whether it lasts two hours or 12. He goes home thinking, 'I've just met a madman.' The second time he meets John, he gets to laughing. And the third time, he's hooked. Just like the rest of us.

"John Hale is driven by an almost supernatural desire to help people. He's angry about what he considers phoniness, bullshit,

*John Hale in 1986.* (Dennis Hellawell)

two-faced people, and hypocrisy. In Washington, D.C., where I lived for a long time, people won't let you become part of their lives. They won't let you become addicted to them.

"I mean, you can get addicted to John Hale."

John Hale was born in Canton, a small rural town in upstate New York. His grandfather was a internationally-renowned judge and chairman of the board of trustees of St. Lawrence University; his mother was an Irish beauty; and his father was an eminent Harvard-educated lawyer and later a judge in St. Lawrence County.

Every night at bedtime, his father would read John and his brother stories of King Arthur and Robin Hood. He steeped his sons in the lore of gallantry and fairness.

He also told John never to be a lawyer.

"When I asked him why not he said, 'Because every morning you get up and shave and you have to look in the mirror. And, sometimes, you don't like what you see.'"

As a result, John grew up "favoring the underdog." He'd always dance with the wallflowers and coach the kids with two left feet.

"I felt it wasn't right that

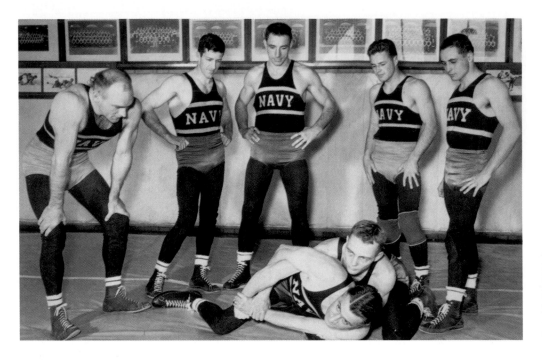

Left: *An Olympic Finalist in 1952, John Hale, middle, is surrounded by past and present Navy wrestling team captains, four of whom were Olympians. Captain Joe Henson, second from left, won the bronze medal in Helsinki in 1952.*
Below: *Commander Hale.*
(U.S. Navy photographer)

somebody should be left out, because she or he wasn't as pretty or as athletic or as talented. It made me angry when people ridiculed others."

On the one hand, John is a rough and ready man. He has broad shoulders, a salt-and-pepper beard, and an anger that lies just beneath the surface. Well past the age of 60, when old wrestlers are long retired, he's been known to back up his anger by punching out some rabble-rouser half his age, taking him by the seat of the pants, and throwing him down the stairs. On the other hand, John is full of Old World charm and courtly manners, a barroom troubadour who quotes Shakespeare and Kipling with ease.

A foxy young artist named Wanda Seamster calls John Hale "the last of the Clark Gables."

It doesn't matter whether a woman is old or young, fat or skinny, well-endowed or flat as a board, John grabs her, kisses her, and tells her she has "beautiful tits."

"He's not afraid of getting slapped," says Wanda. "He knows it's worth it. Young men think it's John's age that allows him to get away with it. It's not. It's his attitude. He kisses all the women, not just the young and pretty ones. He makes all women feel great. And he talks

*When war broke out in Korea, the Navy called him back into service. As a former captain of the Navy wrestling team, he called his old coach—"How about a shot for the Olympics before I ship out to sea?" He trained for a place on the 1952 U.S. Olympic wrestling team, narrowly losing by one match in the final qualifying rounds. His opponent in that match went on to win the gold medal in Helsinki.*

to them, you know, like they're real people."

In high school, little Johnny Hale was the runt of the second-string football team. Desperate to be a big hero, he elected to stay for a fifth year of high school so he could get a shot at playing quarterback. When the first-string quarterback broke his leg, Johnny Hale was sent into the game. He picked up the ball and ran 93 yards for a touchdown, a record that lasted for 20 years. That was, as he says, the first "spectacular event" of his life. The other was winning the Eastern Intercollegiate Championships in 1944, proving that in his weight division he was the best wrestler in the United States.

After graduation from the U.S. Naval Academy and two years of active service, John arrived in Alaska.

They called him "The Wild Man of Nancy Lake." It was 1947. He was 25 years old, lean and wiry, with jet black hair and a deep gravel voice. Originally, he was headed for South Africa. Somehow, he wound up working in a gold mine near Fairbanks, Alaska. Two Athabascan Indians, Shem and Billy Pete, wanted to take him in search of "the lost Nikolai Lode," a mythical storehouse of gold buried deep in interior Alaska.

"It was a dark and dirty job, but somebody had to do it," grins John with one of his favorite lines.

But he wasn't fooled. He just liked to go fishing with them and swap stories. Since their little cabin stood on the banks of Nancy Lake, he moved up there for the winter and staked out a homestead on the peninsula. The only other person who lived near the lake was an old Russian trapper named Mike Ardaw, a former officer in the Tsar's cavalry, who had once hunted Siberian tigers and wrestled wolves to death.

Nancy Lake is 65 miles along the railroad from Anchorage to Fairbanks. The tracks lie across the water about a half a mile from John's homestead property. In 1947, there was no road and no people. Just muskeg, the lake, swamp spruce, tundra, and three friends—two Indians and one Russian.

Painstakingly through that winter, John cut, peeled, notched, and hoisted logs according to the instructions in a little paperback volume of *How to Build A Log Cabin.*

"The key to homesteading in my case was the more incompetent you were, the more people helped you. I wasn't lazy. I was trying hard. But what the hell did I know? All I knew was how to read," says John, who was forever getting lost on his own homestead, much to the amusement of his friends. He would spend hours in the dark winter nights looking for his cabin. To make matters worse, he always sprinted everywhere. So he could get lost faster than most.

After three years in Alaska homesteading and fishing, the young midshipman headed back to New York's Columbia University for a graduate degree in business. He married into one of the wealthy New York blue-blooded families.

"Sunken Orchard," the family estate, was on Long Island near "Sagamore Hill," home of the Teddy Roosevelts. Chauffeurs

*"The key to homesteading in my case was the more incompetent you were, the more people helped you. I wasn't lazy. I was trying hard. But what the hell did I know? All I knew was how to read," says John, who was forever getting lost on his own homestead, much to the amusement of his friends.*

*John's homestead cabin at Nancy Lake. (Hale Collection)*

drove the wealthy around in elegant Caddies and Rollses with the estate names embossed on the side. Not to be outdone, John, with his rebellious brand of humor, drove a Ford station wagon on which he had painted in similarly elegant gold lettering: "Shoeshine." He and his wife Dorothy lived on the third floor of her father's mansion where the servants once shined the shoes.

At the time, John was wrestling at the New York Athletic Club and working construction.

When war broke out in Korea, the Navy called him back into service. As a former captain of the Navy wrestling team, he called his old coach—"How about a shot for the Olympics before I ship out to sea?" He trained for a place on the 1952 U.S. Olympic wrestling team, narrowly losing by one match in the final qualifying rounds. His opponent in that match went on to win the gold medal in Helsinki.

At the Naval Academy, John was voted "the most colorful athlete." He was famous for putting on spectacular shows. He'd use all kinds of fancy holds, such as airplane spins with a half-Nelson crotch or flying long-arm drags. He was so good he could pin his opponents without using any hands, by wearing them down, and then slapping a figure-four head scissors on them.

"You'd try not to humiliate the other guy you're wrestling by running through a series of holds which I could easily have done. You always made it look like he could almost get away," says John, who was nicknamed by his coach "Leaders and Tendons" because that's all that stood out on his gaunt, sinewy frame.

"When you're wrestling, you're always hungry and thirsty," says John, wincing with the pain of that memory. Quoting from Shakespeare, he continues, 'I fear yon Cassius, he has a lean and hungry look.'

"Look at Olympic wrestlers. Their eyes are hollowed out. They have sunken cheeks. They're gaunt, dehydrated people. They look like the walking dead. You go to spit and only bubbles come out of your mouth. It's always a desperate struggle to make weight.

"All your senses get highly tuned. You wrestle better when you're starved. You're faster and more responsive. You're right on the edge. A pin drops and your ears pop up involuntarily. You're like an animal hunting for food. You dream about food. That's all you ever think about.

"My freshman coach was a former Olympic wrestler—Karl Kitt. He made a pledge when he was wrestling and dying of thirst that when he stopped wrestling he would never again walk by a drinking fountain for as long as he lived. To this day—he must be in his late 70s now—he's kept that promise. Wherever he is, if he sees a fountain, he'll go over, lean down, and at least let the water touch his lips."

In the Navy, John was a wrestling hero. He also had high "grease" marks, a rating system for an officer's ability to command. With his enormous energy, he had no trouble getting his men all fired up. But like the classic image of the sailor, he is bow-legged. He'll never forget the time he was passed over for promotion as battalion commander in his first year at the Naval Academy, because, as his senior officer confided, "John, you walk so funny. I just couldn't put you out in front."

"I led a pretty ragged existence in the military. Actually, it's a miracle I made it to the rank of commander and didn't get kicked out. I was always making up songs, playing guitars, doing happy-hour shows, asking embarrassing questions, and sort of pushing people to the edge a little," says John with a twinkle in his eyes.

In 1967, John returned to Alaska, ostensibly to sell the homestead property. Taxes on the land were high. But he never went back to New England. He didn't fit in. Constrained too

*John photographed himself at Point Possession in 1948 after he shot and skinned his first (and only) bear. The bear had just eaten a whole summer's catch of John's smoked salmon. (Hale Collection)*

*John once described his image of a true Alaskan: "A person who has built something with his own hands and is never overly concerned about money or possessions. You can sign a contract with him by shaking his hand. It's a person who leaves his door open and, when he does you a favor, he asks nothing in return."*

much by society, his wild streak breaks loose. He's always been more a man of the people than a man of the privileged class.

Living in the homestead cabin once again near the Little Susitna River, he spent his evenings and Sundays singing outrageous and funny songs for a couple of beers at the Willow Trading Post, a tumbled down old bar on the side of the railroad tracks. He delighted in making up parodies of popular tunes and spicing them up with Alaska characters. Strains of such immortal compositions as "Weeping Willowville" or "Susitna Sue" could often be heard floating through the starry wilderness nights.

### WEEPING WILLOWVILLE
*(To the tune of "Margaritaville")*

*I couldn't get up.*
*My pickup won't start up.*

*My waterbed's frozen,*
*I feel like I'm dead.*
*But next year I'm smarter*
*I'll fill it with Vodka*
*When I get thirsty,*
*I'll drink from my bed.*

*Wasting away again*
*In Weeping Willowville*
*Chasing down my shots*
*With cold Oly beer.*
*Some people claim*
*It's the booze that's to blame*
*But it's a woman*
*Got me drinking here.*

### SUSITNA SUE
*(To the tune of "Sioux City Sue")*

*I drove a herd of caribou*
*That was my fondest boast*
*That's how I came to be*
*At the Willow Trading Post*
*I met a girl from Nancy Lake*
*Her eyes were big and blue*
*I asked her what her name was*
*She said, "Susitna Sue."*

*Susitna Sue, Susitna Sue,*
*Her hair is brown*
*Her eyes are blue*
*I'd swap my old skidoo for you.*
*Susitna Sue, Susitna Sue*
*There ain't no gal as true*
*As my sweet Susitna Sue.*

"The first time I met John Hale, he was living at his cabin at Nancy Lake," says Don

*John and his homestead buddies—Happy Jack Smith and Russian Mike Ardaw. (Ted Bell)*

Markle, an affable young man whose father bought John's homestead.

"I saw this crazy man standing in the front of a double-ender pontoon boat which was a landing craft—that's how he got around the lake. John would fire up the motor and take off across the lake like a bat out of hell. The only way it would run was wide-open. It had no tiller. So when John wanted to turn, he ran to the front of the boat. To go left, he'd lean to the left. To go right, he'd lean to the right. He had that boat plumb full of girls and was roaring across the lake. That's the first time I met John Hale."

John once described his image of a true Alaskan: "A person who has built something with his own hands and is never

*By his own definition, John Hale is a true Alaskan. He'd give someone the shirt off his back. And if you are one of John's inner circle, he'll give the shirt off your back too.*

*John was city manager of Aniak in 1984 and coach of Aniak's wrestling team, "The Half-breeds." (Hale Collection)*

overly concerned about money or possessions. You can sign a contract with him by shaking his hand. It's a person who leaves his door open and, when he does you a favor, he asks nothing in return. Someone like Happy Jack Smith. If you'd go to his place and happened, for instance, to admire one of his rifles, he'd say, 'Take it!' And you'd have a hard time trying to leave without taking it."

By his own definition, John Hale is a true Alaskan. He'd give someone the shirt off his back. And if you are one of the chosen few in John's inner circle,

he'll give the shirt off your back too.

He's thrived on a diversity of jobs in Alaska from construction worker on the North Slope and fisherman in Cook Inlet to director of the state's energy program and manager of the Alaska State Fair. He was the founder, morning disc jockey, and salesman of Alaska's most "eclectic" radio station. He's run The Great Land Games, coached athletic teams, managed political campaigns, even been a political candidate himself ("Give 'Em Hale In The Senate!").

For three years, beginning at

the age of 59, he was city manager of Aniak, an Eskimo and Indian community on the banks of the Kuskokwim River, 300 air miles west of Anchorage. He took the job because he liked the name of their basketball team—"The Half-breeds."

"I'm impressed by any town that can have a sense of humor about itself."

In 1987, he endured a stormy vote by the Matanuska-Susitna (Mat-Su) Borough, the third largest borough government in the state of Alaska, to become its manager. Its history of wild politics and sinking morale left most residents of Alaska calling it "The Mad Zoo Boro."

As one newspaper observed, ". . . officials may be in for a heck of a ride if they intend to keep a tight rein on John Hale. Exuberant and unconventional, the newly appointed manager has been called a 'loose cannon' and 'an unguided missile'—and that's by his friends."

As one savvy political adviser noted, "John's a firm believer in the old theory that government is there to serve. I feel sorry for the first person who comes in with nine reasons why something can't be done. There's going to be a Hale storm."

John Hale would have been one of the richest men in Alaska

*"Think of the possibilities! He's a brilliant, lovable eccentric who has an incredible knack for getting things done. If John Hale were governor, god knows what would happen."*

today. But he gave it all away— land, houses, cars, money. As one longtime friend said, "He's the perfect politician. He can never be corrupted by wealth."

At age 67, he owns nothing. Even approaching the twilight of his years, material things don't mean anything to him. What he loves are words, poems, stories, music, and songs.

The last thing he had left to give away was free music and he did it with glee over the air waves from KABN, the radio station built by his Harvard-educated son, who sold out and left his father to manage the venture. John called it "the pirate radio station." He loved it. As the morning DJ for several years, he commanded a captive audience. It was simple. Every day he made up a "hit list" of his friends, neighbors, and acquaintances. Then he'd say something outrageous about them on the air. People had to tune into KABN to defend themselves.

"We were the best radio station in Alaska, because we

*A Barroom Troubadour: One of the Commander's many original musical compositions is sung by a wild assortment of comrades. From left to right, Norm Cohen, Jim Souby, Hale, and Jeffrey "Mr. Rock and Roll" Macktaz.*
(Nan Elliot)

weren't radio people. We were people people," says John.

It is an illuminating statement from the Commander. Unlike most politicians and bureaucrats who tend to think of the public they serve as a large unidentified mass of opinion, John Hale thinks of the public and sees individual faces.

For the last 10 years, all his friends, a motley assortment of old rednecks and young liberals, have said, "Oh, wouldn't it be grand and wouldn't it be fun if John Hale were governor?"

"He'd set the state on its ear," grins one young admirer.

"Think of the possibilities! He's a brilliant, lovable eccentric who has an incredible knack for getting things done. If John Hale were governor, god knows what would happen."

Like many who have fallen under the Commander's charismatic pied piper spell, cartoonist Billy Spear concludes in his John Hale adventure comic book: "John is one of those rare people who makes this nutty biological experiment worth the candle. When I grow up, I want to be just like John Hale."

# 11

# "I Saw Here Greatness..."

**Y**ou have to have a soul in everything you do . . . or you are nothing," says the warm, animated little Italian lady who adopted this state as her home more than 30 years ago and it hasn't quite recovered yet.

Lidia Selkregg has been an adviser to the governors of Alaska and to the president of the United States. A former professor at the University of Alaska, she has lectured and taught throughout America and Europe, written books, and served as a local politician for years.

The two things that kindle her inner fires are teaching and politics.

But as someone once remarked, "Lidia could never speak in the stylized language of a politician or bureaucrat because, no matter how hard she tries, her hands start flying and her emotions get in the way."

At one meeting of the governor's policy advisory council, for example, Lidia, in the midst of a heated debate, grew exasperated with the council for its slowness in

*Lidia Selkregg in Anchorage: "We had just arrived and before we knew, we had a freezer full of moose and salmon and caribou. The generosity was incredible." (Nan Elliot)*

reaching a decision. She abruptly stood up in the middle of someone else's soliloquy. In a lilting theatrical moment, she announced, "The council is fiddling, while Rome is burning!" With Italian pomp and circumstance, she marched out of the room.

As emotions are unpredictable, so is Lidia. She has stirred controversy, exasperated people, made them think, made them laugh, made them angry, and then smothered them with love. She has a lot to say and she loves to talk. She dances verbal circles around most people because when she runs out of English, she just starts over in Italian. And if she forgets your name upon occasion, it really doesn't matter because she hugs and kisses you and worries over you like a Latin grandmother. She thinks of Alaska as one big extended family—*her* family.

Born in Florence, Italy, in 1920, Lidia spent her teenage years in Tunisia in northern Africa when it was a French protectorate.

"Tunis was very cosmopolitan," she remembers. "Our neighbors on one side were British and on the other side Russian. My mother was a teacher in an Italian school in Tunis during the latter years of Mussolini's dictatorship. She was a strong anti-fascist. She would often say, 'This man cannot conquer education. When I close the door to my classroom, I am the teacher. And I will teach the students what I think is right for them to learn.'"

Those words and philosophy had a tremendous impression on Lidia. As an educator, Lidia feels it was her mother's determination in the face of a repressive system that taught her to be a free thinker and enabled her to encourage others today.

In 1938, Lidia returned to the University of Florence to study for her doctorate in natural sciences, which she received in 1942. Those were also the war years. Much of her time was spent in simply surviving and helping others to survive. She joined the student resistance movement. In the final days of the war, she could hear German voices out the front window of her apartment and watch the American tanks approaching out the back window.

Water was at a premium. "Water is so important psychologically," Lidia explains, which is why as a scientist she says she specialized in ground water geology.

"Our water supply had been cut off. Luckily, there were a few

*In the final days of the war, she could hear German voices out the front window and watch the American tanks out the back.*

> *"I don't want to be chauvinistic. Men are probably very good as soldiers. But they're not very good as preservationists of society. They can say, 'If there's no water, then don't worry about it. If there's no water, then we go without.'"*

people with wells in their backyards. For hours I would pump water for old people and for families like us. Then I'd take my flask back home to mother and we learned to conserve water. Water conservation is one fantastic thing. It's amazing what you can do with a flask of water. You can take a shower, bathe yourself, collect the water in a tub to wash your clothes, and then you can put it in the toilet.

"From this survival concept, you see so many different things," says Lidia. "I don't want to be chauvinistic. Men are probably very good as soldiers. But they're not very good as preservationists of society. They can say, 'If there's no water, then don't worry about it. If there's no water, then we go without.' They don't realize that cleanliness is one of the most important things for people. You have to continue basic society survival or you become more and more hopeless. Women are really preservationists of life. I saw women do incredible things."

After the war, there were many American soldiers still left in Italy. Lidia described herself then as a young woman who loved people. But the war had been "an overpowering tragedy." She was not bitter. Yet she could not go to parties and be joyful. Her mother worried about her. A friend convinced her one evening to go to a dance held by the American soldiers.

"They were all dressed up. They were supposed to look their best with little gloves here and a hat there, just so," remembers Lidia, recreating the scene with animated gestures. "They were all blonde and tall. I thought, 'My god, they're all the same. They look like an advertisement.' And then . . . one guy walked in. I should have known. It was Fred. This guy had no necktie and his shirt had a big cut on the sleeve. He was next to a little fellow with a big camera.

"I said, 'My god, there is one human being here.' And that was Fred. Fred was a fantastic dancer, too, and he loved Florence."

Lidia's eyes sparkle as the story continues amidst the laughter, words tumbling out faster and faster, heavily laced with her wonderful Italian accent.

"Language is not my great forte. I just don't like languages. I spoke French, but only because I had lived in Tunisia. So when we started dancing, I asked if he knew French and he said, 'Oui.'" He agreed with me on everything. When I went home, I said,

'Mother, I met this fantastic American. I talked all sorts of social and philosophical things and he agreed with me. This man has such a tremendous deep conscience.' But later I realized that Fred doesn't know any French. And I didn't know much English. So when he would speak, I would say, 'Oh, yes' and Fred thought 'What a nice fantastic young Italian woman. She agreed with me on everything.'

"You see," continues Lidia, laughing, "We thought we had agreed, but we hadn't even communicated."

Still, it was magic. Unless they tried to meet by telephone, which of course was a disaster. Undaunted, they were married in 1945. Two years later, Fred brought his bride to the United States, eventually settling in a small town in Illinois. Lidia remembers being frightened because she didn't know the language very well or the country. But she was trained to have a career. Her mother came from Italy to visit and take care of the grandchildren. She gently nudged Lidia out the door saying, "Now you go out, baby, and come back with a job."

Lidia returned as a professor of geology at the local university. "But the town was very conser-

vative. When Fred ran for local office, he was the only Democrat to put his name on the ballot in years. We felt if we didn't move, we would be there forever— stilted people, conforming, conforming, conforming."

It was 1958, the year before Alaska statehood, when they packed up and moved north. They decided Fairbanks was too cold. Juneau was too wet. Anchorage seemed just right, on the map at least, surrounded by mountains and the sea.

When they finally arrived, Lidia was shattered. "The ocean had no waves."

The city is situated on the edge of Cook Inlet, which has the second highest tides in the world. When the water retreats twice a day, it exposes a less-than-scenic expanse of mud. The bluffs where Lidia planned to build her home overlooking the ocean were unstable and prone to earthquake damage. The "flap-jack houses" and "ticky-tacky buildings" along downtown Fifth Avenue reminded her of the town she had traveled thousands of miles to escape. She was ready to get in the car and turn back.

"But I loved the people. The first year was fantastic. We met interesting people everywhere— artists, real estate agents, restau-

*"Some of the early laws were very progressive. I saw here greatness, an opportunity for greatness. This town was a little town. But it was the most involved town I ever saw. Public meetings were broadcast on the radio. When somebody had something to say, he rushed down to testify. These people were in touch with each other. It was fantastic."*

rant owners, clothing clerks, politicians. And they absorb us. We had never found people more friendly. We had just arrived and before we knew, we had a freezer full of moose and salmon and caribou. The generosity was incredible. People took out-of-state checks and store clerks gave us things and just said 'Come back and pay later.'

"We thought, 'Here is a society of people who trust each other.'

"Some of the early laws were very progressive. I saw here greatness, an opportunity for greatness. This town was a little town. But it was the most involved town I ever saw. Public meetings were broadcast on the radio. When somebody had something to say, he rushed down to testify. These people were in touch with each other. It was fantastic.

"You're grabbed by this place. Maybe you can do this everywhere. But everywhere there are so many people, you're lost. Here there is so much space. If I want to be in the wilderness, I can be there. Yet last night I was in a fancy hotel with chandeliers, jade stairs, and fine French food. This is a place where you can still blend these two things."

Six years after Lidia and Fred drove into town, the largest earthquake in the history of North America struck Alaska in full force. It was the Friday before Easter, a peaceful but chilly spring day. Snow was lightly falling. Schools were out for vacation. Businesses had just closed. People were slowly meandering home from work, perhaps stopping first to have a beer or two. Nothing seemed so unusual. At 5:36 p.m., the calm was shattered. A terrifying force let loose. The ground began to roll and shake violently. For hundreds of miles, the earth ripped open, buildings toppled, pavement heaved, and houses collapsed.

For months, there had been several little quakes leading up to the big one. At the time, Lidia was working for the Alaska State Housing Authority (ASHA) as a planner and geologist. She had just returned from a trip to southeast Alaska. Fred was at home. Friends were visiting. All of a sudden, the ground began to roll and shake and kept rolling. They waited for it to stop and then realized, "My god, this is the real thing." They rushed out barefoot into the snow.

"The waves were coming from north to south," remembers Lidia. "The ground was rolling in four- to five-foot waves. This

**The largest earthquake in the history of North America struck Alaska in full force the Friday before Easter, 1964. At 5:36 p.m., "all hell broke loose."**

*Fourth Avenue, Anchorage, after the 1964 earthquake. (Ward Wells Collection, Anchorage Museum of History and Art)*

*"The waves were coming from north to south. The ground was rolling in four- to five-foot waves. This house looked like a boat at sea. Downtown, my office collapsed. If I had been there, I would have been killed."*

Lidia straddles a fissure left by the '64 quake. She was one of the top scientists in the field immediately following the devastation. *(Selkregg Collection)*

**Above:** *The port of Seward was on fire following the quake. (Anchorage Museum of History and Art)*

**Left:** *The earthquake measured 8.6 on the Richter scale, toppling houses and twisting steel rails. (Alaska Railroad Collection, Anchorage Museum of History and Art)*

house looked like a boat at sea. Downtown, my office collapsed. If I had been there, I would have been killed."

Alaska was declared a national disaster area. While others were jumping into the breach to provide medical services, food, and relief, Lidia was put in charge of the geological evaluation of what had happened. She put out an appeal over the radio to the scientific community. By 9 a.m. Monday, she had rallied 40 scientists with their maps and compasses. They began a systematic mapping of the cracks and measuring of earth movement. Lidia's ultimate job was to plan for the safe rebuilding of homes and businesses.

"Planners, architects, and engineers should be worried about public safety. We are in the highest seismic area in the world. We have tremors all the day," she says. "You can track all that activity with computers now and map where those little earthquakes are. There are two gaps—one in the Aleutian chain and one around Yakutat. These are very hot spots. When they go, there will be a tremendous release of energy."

As a planner, Lidia believes she is an artist. She visualizes things before they happen. Planning, she says, is a system of relationships. One of her most passionate concerns is the relationship of people to their government, the participation of citizens in decisions governing their lives and their future.

"I doubt I would run for political office in any other state," she reflects. "You either have to be a political animal or have a family very rich. Maybe in Alaska it will be true in the future. But I arrived when Alaska was a baby and watched it grow.

"It is the only place in the world where you can see the governor having a sandwich by himself in some restaurant or meet your senators on the street. The relation of people to government is so important. Yet only 30 percent of the people here are permanent. The rest are the come-and-go-out. They don't want to stay. They want jobs, to make money fast, and go. They don't give a damn about Alaska. They want it now. This has a tremendous impact on policy decisions. The mistake made by politicians is that they respond to this temporary group. The people who stay, those are the ones who care about Alaska. They want a beautiful city and protection of the open spaces.

"In Alaska we have a chance to do things differently, to do things better."

*"I doubt I would run for political office in any other state. You either have to be a political animal or have a family very rich. Maybe in Alaska it will be true in the future. But I arrived when Alaska was a baby and watched it grow."*

(Nan Elliot)

But the planner, visionary and lover of people in Lidia worries that Alaskans are not carving the future of their state in an innovative, creative way, but rather importing old ideas and maybe if the state continues down this dull but well-traveled road that Alaska will begin to look like every place else. It will lose its freshness and uniqueness.

"We are talking of a sub-continent which has the complexities of many, many countries," she says emphatically. "And we are treating it as if everything has to be the same from the Arctic to the panhandle. We should recognize regional differences and reflect that. You find different governments from Norway to Spain, which is the same kind of distance that covers Alaska, but we have a monolithic approach here. This is the frustration of lots of Alaskans. The ability is here. But we have been educated or conditioned to conform. This has not allowed for all these free thinkers, free brains, and free ideas to flow.

"I think the people are ready, but is the government?"

"I'D SWAP MY OLD SKIDOO FOR YOU"

# 12

## The Channel Bowl ("Roll With The Punches") Cafe

*Just a regular day at the Channel Bowl Cafe in Juneau. From left to right, Bobbi Beery, Teri Tibbett, Laurie Berg, Teeny Metcalfe, Ben Grussendorf, and Barb Murray.*
*(Mark Kelley)*

On the banks of Gastineau Channel in downtown Juneau stands a rather ordinary brown building. But past the gigantic bowling pin and through the double doors is the home of a once-disreputable sport and a revamped greasy spoon that is tickling the funny bone of Alaska's capital city.

Not so long ago, bowling was ranked with booze and billiards, the sole purview of gamblers and lowlifes. But in the 1950s, it burst upon the small-town American scene with a popularity undiminished today.

In the 1980s, the Channel Bowl bowling alley gained a new reputation. Not, as they say in bowling lingo, for its fudge balls and splashers, but for its little hole-in-the-wall diner, the Channel Bowl Cafe. While the pins are dancing and tumbling after Deloris or Sammy or Junior rolls a turkey down pie alley, the champion roller of wits, Laurie Berg, is flipping burgers (or "Bergers") merely a gutter ball away in the Channel Bowl ("Roll With The

Punches") Cafe. It's OK, she's got a license for mirth. She's a graduate with a "Bachelor's Degree in Rhymes." Her kindergarten diploma hangs by the door. Beside it is a photo of little boys in cowboy hats around a birthday cake with the warning: "No dessert until you clean your plate!"

A step into the cafe is like a step back in time.

"Waaaaaay back," says the sassy young blonde from Minnesota, chewing and snapping on an imaginary wad of gum. Way back to the days when the music was swing and the diner was king.

"She's a wiseacre, that one," mumbles an old-timer at the counter. He is bent over a steaming cup of coffee while the 1930s toe-tapping music of Louis Alter's "You Turned the Tables on Me" plays in the background. "Smarty pants, that's what we said in my day. But hell, if she didn't razz you, you'd think she was mad at you or something."

"How'd you like the toast, George?" she calls from the cash register.

"Uh, yeah. Uh, good. It was good," replies George.

"Great toast, isn't it?" she announces to the motley crew at the counter with a kind of half giggle. "Best in town," she says

*The Berg-er-meister.* (Nan Elliot)

as she flips a couple of fancy pancakes. "I don't know what we do to it here . . ." she continues, as one hand reaches over and pops up another four slightly charred pieces. "Must be the timing." She fixes someone with a meaningful look and then disintegrates into another half laugh as she speeds over to the oven to pull out about six dozen of Berg's Famous Chocolate Chunk Cookies.

A not-so-young whippersnapper saunters in the door, grinning. "Is there a cook here yet?"

The retort comes fast. "Go sit in the bowling alley, Jim, and throw some quarters at the pop

*Enter, but don't check
your wits at the door.
The action is fast.
And the humor is
flying. Friendly insults
go hurtling by. Fry
cooks and customers,
everyone jumps into
the act. This is a "full
service" cafe. The
place is tiny—nine bar
stools and three tables.
You're never a
stranger for long.*

machine. There's no coffee in here for you."

To a customer at the counter she gives the aside: "I want him to come back on his knees. And treat this place with a little respect."

Two young yuppie women in raincoats and Hermes scarves belly up to the counter. "A Mount Jumbo, please."

Laurie turns from the grill and over the noise of the splattering grease calls back, "Just one order?"

The shorter woman raises an eyebrow. "Do you think we'd actually *risk* getting two?"

Enter, but don't check your wits at the door. The action is fast. And the humor is flying. Friendly insults go hurtling by. Fry cooks and customers, everyone jumps into the act. This is a "full service" cafe. The place is tiny—nine bar stools and three tables. You're never a stranger for long.

"Breakfast? Did you say *breakfast*?" snaps Sophie Zimmer-"woman," with her punk hairdo and hands on her apron. "It's one in the afternoon, you bimbo, why didn't you get up when everyone else did?"

The fisherman at the counter pulls his cap down over his ears and grins. Clearly a regular, he turns to his neighbor with cocky

assurance and says, "The great thing about this place is that you can come here—and if you beg, I mean *beg*—you can get breakfast any time of the day."

Fast-talking, fast-walking Laurie Berg buzzes each table with the coffee pot and plates filled with mountains of food. She's usually dressed in rolled-up sweat pants or a country cotton frock, which her mom makes for her back on the farm in Minnesota. Her hair is swept up in artful disarray. She's a one-liner with an offbeat sense of humor. Words are her forte. And she loves to put slight kinks in the old variations.

The menu and name of the Channel Bowl Cafe vary with her daily whimsy. Don't rely on the printed menus. They are merely souvenirs, part of the art deco decor. Just like the photo of the dead Barbie doll and the toasters hanging by their cords over the red neon Coca-Cola sign in the window. What you see is not what you get. What's happening is all up on the blackboard behind the counter and next to the grill. The day's specials are: Mediocre Meat Loaf; Minnesota-strone Soup; Really Good Chicken; and Omelets with Not-So-Hot Sauce."

The motto of the place is "(mostly) Decent Food."

Today it is the Cannibal Cafe. "Eat at your own risk." On Halloween it was the Channel Ghoul Cafe. And on Passover, the Channel Matzo Cafe. When politics get racy, it's the Channel Scam Cafe. Last Monday, it was the Channel Snooze Cafe. Tuesday rolled around and it was the Channel Small-Talk Cafe; Wednesday, the Channel You-Got-All-Day Cafe; and on Thursday, after Laurie got a long-distance phone call from some poor would-be tourist in New York City asking for reservations at "her little lodge," the name changed to the Channel Bowl Cafe and Hunting Lodge. She took the reservation deadpan. Come next August, there's going to be one mighty surprised lady from the Bronx arriving in Juneau on holiday.

The Channel Bowl Cafe is, as one customer says, a den of political rumor and intrigue, where, if you bad-mouth the commissioner, you'll always be overheard.

On any given day, there's an odd mixture of clientele: school bus drivers, retirees, beauticians, bowlers, fishermen, politicians, legislative aides, the governor's cabinet members, even the governor himself.

You can order off the blackboard, if you dare, or one of the items on the regular menu: a Mount Jumbo, "breakfast to match our mountain"; Bill's Fancy Pancakes, named for Bill Ross, a pancake devotee and former commissioner of environmental conservation; Warren's Special, because Warren was "nobody in particular"; a Mondale burger and Ferraro fries, only available in national election year 1984; and Rocky's Memorial Breakfast, named for Rocky Gutierrez from Sitka, the short-lived commissioner of transportation in Juneau, before he quit to go home.

"Rocky made some comment to the newspaper here that you couldn't get a good cheap breakfast in town—not like you could in Sitka," says Laurie Berg. So she wrote a letter to the editor saying the Channel Bowl Cafe served one. And she named it after Rocky.

"He said he could get two eggs, meat, a pancake, and potatoes for $3.50. So I did it here. Then a lot of fishermen were in here one day wondering where in the world Rocky Guiterrez eats in Sitka, because they've never been able to get a cheap breakfast there."

Laurie bursts into peals of laughter. "After he left Juneau, it became Rocky's Memorial Breakfast."

*Today, it is the Cannibal Cafe. "Eat at your own risk." On Halloween, it was the Channel Ghoul Cafe. And on Passover, the Channel Matzo Cafe. When politics get racy, it's the Channel Scam Cafe . . . and on Thursday, after Laurie got a long-distance phone call from some poor would-be tourist in New York City asking for reservations at "her little lodge," the name changed to the Channel Bowl Cafe and Hunting Lodge.*

*Laurie Berg is a one-liner with an offbeat sense of humor.* (Nan Elliot)

"Hey, Laurie, how long ya gonna be in town this time?" calls out one customer. Another young guy at the counter adds: "You know, some people would call your lifestyle . . ."

" . . . irresponsible," sings Laurie, filling in the sentence and dancing around with her spatula, "Call me irresistible . . ." Then she breaks down giggling again. Another cafe devotee, Melinda Gruening, a young mother who runs a wilderness lodge at Baranof Warm Springs Bay near Sitka, confides with a grin to her luncheon companion, "A lot of people are green when they think of Laurie's lifestyle."

You see, Laurie just *loves* vacations. Almost all are outside and exuberant, such as helicop-

ter skiing, white water rafting, biking, kayaking, and hiking. Sometimes, she takes off for months at a time. As the old television show used to say, "Have passport. Will travel."

No matter. She has a back-up crew of equally wacky employees.

Teeny Metcalfe, another fast-talking, five-foot blonde with a contagious personality, is the second fastest fry cook on the grill. She has held down the fort on many occasions. She practically opened the place with Laurie.

Teeny was born in Juneau, one of nine children. Her grandmother came north around the turn of the century during the gold rush.

"With nine kids, college was

never mentioned in my family. We couldn't even afford to go to the dentist. If you got a toothache, you put an aspirin in the tooth or, if it was real bad, grandmother would make us gargle with whiskey." Teeny worked as a telephone operator, a cocktail waitress, a bartender, a commercial fisherwoman, and then got several jobs with the state legislature as a page for the House of Representatives, a legislative aide, and sergeant-at-arms.

"But that was a nightmare. You're not working for one guy. You're working for 40 maniacs." She decided politics was not it. So she retired at age 25 to go to college.

"I graduated from college in 1984 and came back to Juneau. I never wanted to be a waitress again. Before I was officially an adult though, I was going to go to New Zealand. I heard that Laurie had just opened a restaurant in the bowling alley. She called me up.

"'No,' I said. 'I'm not working as a waitress in a goddamn bowling alley. I just graduated from college. Only dips work in the bowling alley.'

"And I was right," she laughs. "The next day I was working at the bowling alley. I couldn't believe it. Here I'd just

spent $22,000 on my college education and I come back to Juneau and flip burgers for a living.

"But then people started coming in. The place is tiny and hot and greasy. There's no wall between you and them. They see everything. They see how hard you work. And they treat you, you know, with respect. They even come in here for advice. Because you've got a spatula in your hand, they think you know what you're talking about. It just got funnier and funnier.

"We were so goofy. That's a lot of the appeal. People came in here just to watch the floor show. You see, it's a little left of center, odd, and quick-witted. Laurie's one of seven kids, I'm one of nine, and Barb Murray, another one of the cooks, is one of 10. In a big family, you develop a real quick wit early on for self-defense. Somebody gives you a little flack and you tend to throw it right back at them. And believe me," she laughs, "it's had some fine-tuning over the years.

"All the time, customers volunteer to wash dishes for you and pour coffee. I think they feel privileged just for being let behind the counter."

Even Governor Bill Sheffield cooked in the Channel Bowl the

*Teeny Metcalfe was born in Juneau, one of nine children. Her grandmother came north for the gold rush.*
(Nan Elliot)

*"People come in here just to watch the floor show. You see, it's a little left of center, odd, and quick-witted."*
—Teeny Metcalfe

*Teeny Metcalfe (left), the "second fastest fry cook" at the Channel Bowl, and owner Laurie Berg. (Nan Elliot)*

work out," she flashed the big diamond ring on her finger, "I'm at least a couple thousand dollars ahead."

Even Shirley Dean went back to her job with the Human Rights Commission. She was a vegetarian fry cook with a mission. Under her reign, the diner was the "Channel No-Meat Cafe," featuring "bovine meatloaf and dead fish." Said one customer, "She'd cook meat for you, but only if you *really* wanted it."

It was Shirley who ran over the toaster. With her car. Of course, everyone has a slightly different version. And they're eager to tell. The story bubbles out one winter afternoon at the cafe when the action is slow.

John Greely, once the governor's press secretary and one of the best political reporters in Juneau, is now doing time as a fry cook because he made the mistake of marrying into the wacky Berg family. He sports a black baseball cap, given to him by the owner of the cafe, alias his sister-in-law Laurie Berg. The cap says "I get paid weekly. Damn weakly."

According to John, the mangled toasters hanging by their cords in the window "committed suicide."

Sophie can't wait to "take five," sit down for a quick

week before he left office. Rumor in the cafe was that he needed a job. A fellow from the Salvation Army thrift store next door came over and ate two breakfasts right in a row. "He just loved the whole idea of the governor cooking for *him*," says Laurie.

There are many alumnae Channel Bowl chefs. Teeny went on to staff the Governor's Commission on Children and Youth. Barb Murray now runs a wilderness adventure program for juvenile delinquents she calls "Hoods in the Woods." Teri Tibbett, Alaska's number one recording artist and granddaughter of the famous Metropolitan Opera baritone Laurence Tibbett, gave up the fry cook's apron and returned to her music. J.C. Bradshaw, the glamorous yet funky aerobics instructor, who took a few months spin at the grill, retired to get married. As she whizzed around pouring coffee on one of her days off, she explained with a smile, "Yeah, I'm getting married. But if it doesn't

smoke, and dish the real dirt. "She'll do anything to sit down on the job," calls out speed-shoes Berg with that infectious laugh.

Sophie, too, has a rather quirky past. One should be careful of a chef who once cooked for a now-defunct, supposedly four-star restaurant in Texas called "Arsenic and Old Lace."

"The toasters? Yeah, well . . . they kept shocking us. So we strung them up. The law of the wild west, you know," says Sophie, slowly puffing on her cig.

The two bashed toasters hang by their cords in the front window. Someone stuck plastic roses in them as a memorial and draped them in wreaths of fake cobwebs. The other dysfunctional toasters are stashed downstairs in the basement, fondly known as the "toaster graveyard."

"The toasters are a reminder of the hazards of coming in here," Sophie continues. "Every time one would shock us, Laurie would disappear into the graveyard and get another one that supposedly worked better. But it'd usually only cook toast on one side or something. Now if they start to shock us, we grab them and hold them up to the ones in the window to remind them of what could happen to them." Sophie is

laughing. The customers are laughing. And Laurie is giggling at the grill.

"Laurie left once for Minnesota," Sophie continues, clearly on a roll, "and said if the toaster stopped working while she was gone, she'd buy a new one. So Shirley took it out and ran over it with her car to make sure it was dead. Otherwise, Laurie would just keep popping them down in the toaster graveyard and after a few months they get reborn.

"How would I describe Laurie? She has a sense of style that's, well . . . beyond. We'll just leave it at that."

Laurie can be heard laughing in the background.

In addition to her degree in rhymes, the Berg-er-meister of the Channel Bowl Cafe has a college degree in agricultural economics. Her first foray into the restaurant business was her lunch cart in Juneau called "Standing Room Only." The signs advertised, "Buy a felafel and save the world!" or "Free trip to Mexico with the first $5,000 purchase."

Laurie doesn't stick around long to answer many more questions. She hates talking about herself. And she'd crawl backwards around the block to avoid having her photograph taken.

*In addition to her degree in rhymes, the Berg-er-meister of the Channel Bowl Cafe has a college degree in agricultural economics. Her first foray into the restaurant business was her lunch cart in Juneau called "Standing Room Only." The signs advertised, "Buy a felafel and save the world!" or "Free trip to Mexico with the first $5,000 purchase."*

*Laurie rolls a fudge ball down pie alley.* (Nan Elliot)

But she'll do anything for a joke.

Ask her to pose on her head and she's the prima ballerina. She will two-step out onto a bowling lane with a flourish and flip over on her noggin, legs waving around in the air. She's as famous for her headstands as she is for twirling her fire batons, anytime, anywhere. High up on a mountain, rafting down a river, or on a beached glacial ice berg. The joke is irresistible—a Berg a la berg.

Why is Alaska her home?

"I've grown fond of it," she grins.

Do Alaskans differ from other people?

She starts to giggle that contagious belly-warming laugh. "They eat more." She is consumed with mirth now. Clearly, the customers aren't the only ones to get a bang out of her humor. "And," she says gasping for air, "they walk out on their bills more."

"It's true," confides a cus-tomer. "It's such a friendly place, a lot of people forget to pay the bill. It's just like eating at mom's."

Faster than a speeding bullet, Laurie is off again with her steaming coffee pot, dreaming of her next practical joke. The warm tones of that old swing favorite "Stompin' at the Savoy" float over the sounds of splattering grease. Bud and Betty are burn-ing another string of strikes out in the alley. And, for one brief goofy moment, all seems well with the world.

# 13

# Destination: Glacier Bay

I n 1879, by canoe, the famous naturalist John Muir explored and mapped the awesome ice-filled bay today known as Glacier Bay, one of the jewels of our national parks.

For the old Scot, Alaska was "the morning of creation" where he could hear "the stars singing together." So impressed was he by the wildness and stunning beauty of the country that he urged his readers, "Go to Alaska. Go and See."

One hundred years later, almost to the month, two young men went north to see.

Not by plane (although 50 years after Muir's odyssey here, Alaska would become the "flyingest" state in the union). Not by car. Not by steamer. Not under sail. Instead, they set out from Seattle under misty, gray skies in early June 1979 on two sliding seats, each man pulling on a pair of 10-foot oars in an open wooden dory.

In a 100-year anniversary celebration of Muir's ex-

*Peter McKay: "To Alaskans, nothing seems impossible." (Joel Bennett)*

*Peter, the "Old Salt," misjudges the tides and gets caught high and dry in Gastineau Channel.* (Nan Elliot)

plorations, Peter McKay, then age 27, along with his partner, Dick Luxon, was going to row to Alaska.

The 18-foot boat, a traditional Grand Banks dory design, was painted bright blue with red trim and on the bow the name (and destination) in metallic gold letters read: "Glacier Bay." The cockpit was jammed with 400 pounds of gear from compass and navigational charts to fishing line and junk food.

Pulling about 25 miles a day, they weathered unpredictable and violent storms blowing off the North Pacific Ocean, navigated dangerous tidal currents, battled "quarter-pound mosquitoes," and rowed sometimes 18 hours a day. The last 50 miles into Glacier Bay took them a week, backs braced against 40-mile-an-hour head winds and heavy seas. The final 10 miles, just to test their grit, took eight hours with waves breaking over the bow. When they finally touched ground at the park headquarters in Glacier Bay, they bought a bottle of whiskey and somewhere halfway through it, figured out that in two months they had rowed nearly 1,500 miles.

Reporters loved them. In every small town along the Inside Passage of British Columbia and Alaska, the rowers were instant celebrities. The curious lined up to watch, as one newspaperman observed, "getting vicarious thrills out of promising themselves they would do that some day, secure in the knowledge they never would." After all, the press jockey pointed out:

*He'll go to great extremes and put himself through enormous discomfort to tease someone and never admit he was teasing. Have a discussion about some early explorer getting eaten by cannibals and Peter will remark casually, "God, I hate when that happens." Paddle into seven-foot seas with the rain blowing horizontally and the fog descending into a white-out, and Peter will grin and yell, "Hey, we're in luck. Weather doesn't get much better than this."*

"High adventure reads well, but in practice it is damned uncomfortable."

One insistent reporter kept prodding: OK, sure they learned about bears and mosquitoes and wild seas and tidal rips, but what larger lessons about life were they learning? And Peter responded, flashing that great grin which is his illustrious trademark, "The importance of the rear." (In other words, there can never be too much padding for rowing more than a thousand miles while sliding back and forth on a small metal seat.)

More seriously, he added, "I have also learned that men needn't despair at the lack of new frontiers."

The most impressive feature of Peter's boyish good looks is his wonderful smile. He is a hail-fellow-well-met, willing to lend a helping hand. Still, there's a certain rebelliousness in his spirit. He sports the rumpled Ivy League look with loose-fitting clothes, crumpled button-down Oxford shirts and ties askew. He hates brushing his hair. But he loves stirring the pot, asking casual questions that drop like bombshells.

He'll go to great extremes and put himself through enormous discomfort to tease someone and never admit he

was teasing. Have a discussion about some early explorer getting eaten by cannibals and Peter will remark casually, "God, I hate when that happens." Paddle into seven-foot seas with the rain blowing horizontally and the fog descending into a white-out, and Peter will grin and yell, "Hey, we're in luck. Weather doesn't get much better than this."

Peter without a telephone is like a fish out of water. Once this was a hardship on long wilderness trips. But now he has a marine radio so he can dial his friends from wherever he ends up—whether he's at the top of Mount Jumbo across from the city of Juneau or bobbing around in his boat out in the Gulf of Alaska.

He loves being in the information flow and at home gets a kind of perverse delight at subjecting himself and any guests to a nonsensical media blitz. He'll turn on the television and radio and read the newspaper while at the same time talking on the telephone and trying to cook some gourmet Thai oddity like a garlic and pineapple hors d'oeuvre called "flaming galloping horses."

Peter is a world traveler with a mission. He dreams of expeditions, charts his destinations on the map, plans for months, and then with a marathoner's single-mindedness, he rows, climbs, skis, and, in the final gasp, sometimes crawls his way there. He travels for fun and he travels for work.

In high school, Peter ran cross-country and track and then got into what he calls "a dead sport"—Olympic race walking. He went to college in Boston on a partial athletic scholarship, then dropped out to join the Peace Corps.

"They said, 'Colombia.' I said, 'Sure, let's get the hell out of here.'

"When I got to South America, everything was stripped away from my act. I came from a materialistic culture. These people didn't have much. They enjoyed simple things, family things. They were working on difficult problems, trying to colonize the jungle and raise basic foodstuffs. You see suffering. But you see people getting by. The whole spirit of the Peace Corps is to lend a hand."

That experience launched Peter on a lifelong career working with rural people and dealing with the economics of land. It has also taken him around the globe.

For several years, he lived with Chicano farm workers in California, setting up agricultural

*(Nan Elliot)*

co-ops for the production of strawberries and starting a bilingual radio station. He traveled to the Gambia as a leader for Crossroads Africa, where his group helped villagers build a dam and medical clinic. For three years, he directed an experimental agricultural project in the middle of subarctic Alaska, training Eskimo and Indian people—traditionally hunters and gatherers—to be farmers.

More than anything, Peter loves rowing. "It's always an adventure to be on the water," he says. When he was five years old living on the banks of Lake Erie, there was an old rowboat he'd push into stormy weather with big, scary waves. He was thrilled. Not too smart, but thrilled. He never could paddle the boat back to shore. Fortunately, indulgent fishermen kept rescuing him.

Perhaps that's the appeal of the dory. "It's a classic. The most seaworthy rowboat ever built. It's like a '56 Chevy—reliable and safe," says Peter. "In rough water, it just dances around and feels its way." Under pressure, however, Peter does admit that "sometimes though you can get into trouble."

Strangely enough, the only time Peter and Dick swamped coming up the coast to Alaska was not in the boat. It was in their tent.

In a fit of exhaustion, they flopped on shore after a 12-hour day of pulling on the oars, wolfed down a couple of salmon apiece, and collapsed in their sleeping bags. A small miscalculation. They had pitched their tent below the high tide level on a coast that has some of the highest tides in the world. In the darkest part of the summer night on an island in British Columbia, the sea lapped about the edges of their tent and floated it off on the waves, southward into the shipping lanes of the North Pacific Ocean.

"We were asleep. I remember turning over and feeling it was real comfortable, but also having a sense that something was not quite right. I didn't want to wake up. I was exhausted. I didn't want to deal with anything that was wrong.

Finally, Dick woke up and said, 'Pete, don't move. We're floating.'

"We had seam-sealed the tent five times. It was totally water-proofed. But we were worried about concentrating the weight in any one place, figuring the whole thing would collapse. It was about two in the morning and dark out. We had no idea where we were. Carefully, Dick un-zipped the tent and jumped out into the 40-degree water and pitch dark.

"At first it looked like we were about a mile from shore, but we were only about a foot-ball field away. The tide had lifted up the boat and all our pots and pans. The whole flotilla was floating out. Dick swam the tent to shore. I pulled in the boat. Then we swam around in the dark collecting things. The tide had peaked and had started moving out real fast. If we hadn't have woken up, we would have been swept around the corner into a huge shipping lane. Days later, we had visions of waking up and seeing a big ship bearing down on us. It would have ruined our day.

"Rowing the Inside Passage was really beautiful—narrow channels with forests of dark trees lining the edge, fog on the water, and whales spouting around the boat. From Seattle to

*"Rowing the Inside Passage was really beautiful—narrow channels with forests of dark trees lining the edge, fog on the water, and whales spouting around the boat. From Seattle to Glacier Bay, it was like a slow crescendo as the mountains got higher and the snow got lower down."*

*"It's always an adventure to be on the water," says Peter. (Joel Bennett)*

things. The people are friendly. The politics make it interesting. We're all packed in here up against the mountains. It's pretty easy to keep your finger on the pulse. Besides, living in a rain forest is kind of fun. It has a sort of spiritual cleansing effect. Just when it starts to drive you nuts, it's springtime."

A rural planner, Peter travels to villages throughout southeast and southwest Alaska advising communities on land issues. In the winter, he usually takes a leave of absence to travel the world for a few months. Fluent in Spanish, he'll ramble around the hills of Bolivia or pack his skis to the 16,000-foot level of the Andes. In the summer, he takes off in his wooden dory, following in the footsteps of early-day explorers.

"The funny thing about Alaskans is their self-assuredness. You can't surprise them," says Peter. "No matter what you do—fly to Bali, climb Mt. McKinley, drive a dog team to the North Pole—everything is possible to people here. Whatever's happening—avalanches, earthquakes, plane crashes—nothing surprises them. They take it all in stride."

So when Peter decided one summer to row from Glacier Bay around Cape Spencer north along the exposed coast of the

Glacier Bay, it was like a slow crescendo as the mountains got higher and the snow got lower down.

"When I got to Juneau (the capital of Alaska, about 50 miles south of Glacier Bay) I thought, 'Gee, I'd love to live here.'

"The wilderness is why I came to Alaska," says Peter. "I like the cold. I like the snow. I like the mountains and the ocean. Juneau has all these

*Peter sets off on an early summer morning with Brian Daugherty and his dog, Max, to row 70 miles from Juneau to Glacier Bay—a one- to five-day trip, depending on the seas and weather. (Nan Elliot)*

eastern Gulf of Alaska to Lituya Bay, which has a turbulent and tragic history, a few thought he might die, but no one advised against it.

Along 100 miles of stormy coastline in the Gulf of Alaska from Cape Spencer to Yakutat, Lituya Bay is the only "safe" harbor from the storms. In 1786, the first white man to explore it, a Frenchman named La Perouse, lost two boats "and 21 brave mariners" in the wild waters at the entrance to the bay.

The tides are high, the entrance is very narrow, and the whole North Pacific Ocean flows in and out twice a day, creating serious navigational hazards. In 1958, a huge mass of rock and ice split off from the Fairweather Mountain Range and fell into the bay, creating a wave 1,700 feet high. Three fishing boats were in the bay at the time. One was smashed. Two miraculously survived, one surfing the wave over the spit of land into the Gulf.

Subsequent scientific study showed that Lituya Bay, which lies on the Fairweather fault line, has evidence of such devastating tidal waves every 25 years or so.

As one scientist said, it only needs a volcano to make it a perfect microcosm of geologic hazards on the Pacific coast.

Undaunted, Peter made the journey with a friend who had never rowed before. Rounding Cape Spencer, they got blown six miles out to sea by powerful winds roaring down the Brady Glacier. But they had more fear of bears than wild seas and slept anchored out in the boat more than once. It was May and the snow was still down on the ground. It was particularly cold. This was an endurance trip. But

*Adventures—miserable, ill-fated, thrilling, and exciting—that's what keeps Peter going. "Small adventures," grins Peter. "I don't need to go for the gold like scaling K2 or Annapurna."*

they lived to make it back to Glacier Bay and crash a farewell party for a departing park ranger on board the National Park Service boat.

As one ranger remembers, "Peter was pretty happy to be back. He tied his boat up to the stern of our boat and even though it was sinking in our wake, Peter kept right on drinking beer. Finally, we had to let them off. The last we saw of Peter and Dave they were sitting in a boat half full of freezing water, bailing furiously to stay afloat in the middle of the bay."

Adventures—miserable, ill-fated, thrilling, and exciting— that's what keeps Peter going. "Small adventures," grins Peter. "I don't need to go for the gold like scaling K2 or Annapurna."

In a way, it's like his childhood admiration for tugboat operators. He never wanted to be the captain of a big ship. He always thought "the most honorable profession" would be a tugboat captain.

"You're not going for glory. You're just out on the water, working hard."

# 14

# The Duchy Of Halibut Cove

Clem Tillion was born with his feet in salt water. With yachts and boats tied up to the dock, the family home was always within sound of the whistle buoy.

A descendent of five generations of architects, Clem was once the last of the line of Tillions.

His father designed and built Manhattan Towers, one of the first skyscrapers in New York City, about which a Broadway musical was written. His cousin, a former publisher of the *Wall Street Journal*, still lives on a piece of land in the middle of Manhattan that was deeded to the family by Peter Stuyvesant, governor of New York, in the 17th century when it was called "New Netherland" and ruled as a Dutch colony.

His ancestors were French Huguenots, once spearbearers to the throne.

"Tillion," according to Clem, means "hold the spear." Dressed in his classic red suspenders, the red-haired Tillion

*Diana Tillion navigates her boat, the* Lucky, *through the waters of Halibut Cove.*
Inset: *Clem and Diana Tillion.*
(Nan Elliot)

jokes, "You know, the guy who says, 'Hey chief, they're getting kind of close. You sure you don't want your spear now?'"

By heritage, Clem is part French, Scottish, and English with a generous dollop of Irish blarney and an eighth-part Mohawk Indian. But in his heart, he's all Alaskan—a fisherman and politician.

In his 60s now, he is the patriarch of Halibut Cove, a little colony of fishermen and artists on the south side of Kachemak Bay, across from the small town of Homer. It is an idyllic setting, surrounded by snowy mountains, glaciers, and deep green forests. A seal swims around the dock. A clown-faced puffin flies overhead. The distinctive call of the loon floats over the water. Here the ocean is rich with shrimp, cod, mussels, halibut, salmon, and king crab.

"As far as thrills—yes, I've had some fabulous fishing years. There's no excitement like closing the seine and starting to purse in and realizing you've got more fish in that net than you can hold. There's a thrill you can't find anywhere else. Coming in with all the pumps going and the decks awash is pretty exciting. A good fisherman has to be someone who doesn't mind being uncomfortable, someone who enjoys the thrill of the hunt. It's a heck of a lot of work. It's also a gamble.

"You push all your chips to the middle of the table and ask for a new card every year. People say, 'Oh, he was lucky...' Well, the same ones are lucky every year."

Clem has seen his share of danger in some of the wildest weather the ocean can whip up. "With a boat, you push it to the very edge. And you push it once. Then you have the advantage of knowing that nothing short of that will ever bother you again.

"I survived winds in the channel one time of 112 miles an hour. Trees were coming down. A skiff that we had tied to a buoy stood out and flapped like a flag. It wasn't in the water. It was in the air. I couldn't see out the windows. I was picking up water off the sea to where there was absolutely no visibility. Well, I know I can take that now. But I don't go out there on a full-time basis anymore. I'm too old.

"A few years ago, my son Willy was heading out to the Bering Sea to fish. He said, 'Come on, Dad. You handle the wheel.'

"I said, 'Thanks, but no thanks, Willy. I'm old. I want my martini in the evening and some-

*"As far as thrills—yes, I've had some fabulous fishing years. There's no excitement like closing the seine and starting to purse in and realizing you've got more fish in that net than you can hold. There's a thrill you can't find anywhere else. Coming in with all the pumps going and the decks awash is pretty exciting."*

*—Clem*

*The Tillion home on Ismailof Island in Halibut Cove.* (Nan Elliot)

thing soft and warm alongside me at night.'

"As they used to say, I've seen the elephants." Clem grins. He could have been one of the original little rascals in "Spanky and Our Gang."

When he sees the line doesn't quite register across the generation gap, he elaborates: "It's an old American saying from the Civil War days when Barnum and Bailey first brought an elephant into the circus. People who say they've seen everything, say 'I've seen the elephant.' There's nothing else. Don't feed me a line."

Even when he is speaking se-riously, there is always a gener-ous hint of mischievous delight lurking about Clem's face. De-spite his upper-crust upbringing, he's the rambunctious country cousin. He barely finished a year of high school before dashing off to war, desperately fearful he was going to miss all the action.

"I just loved the war, the fighting, the excitement, things going off . . ." Clem lives on adrenaline rushes. Behind the controls of a boat, his face lights up with a kind of maniacal joy, as he careens over the waves from crest to crest, flaps up and full throttle.

In contrast, his wife Diana is serious and soft-spoken. Nearing 60 years of age, she still has a kind of schoolgirl freshness with her shoulder-length hair and bright eyes. While Clem has the energy of a roaring river rushing over the rocks, Diana has the quiet intensity of a sun-streaked summer evening overlooking calm seas.

She is an artist. And paints in an unusual medium—octopus ink.

The sea influences much of her artwork.

"The ocean is so powerful and unyielding," she says. "You cannot help but be dazzled by it. I use octopus ink to paint things of great intensity. To me, it's a living color, a gift from the sea," says Diana, who has a studio in her home on one end of Ismailof Island in Halibut Cove. Wooden boardwalks run from the large rambling house and its lovely hills of green lawn and flowers to Diana's geodesic dome art gallery on the hill, where her paintings sell to visitors and tourists throughout the summer.

"I can easily paint a painting with one drop of octopus ink. It's so incredibly dense and warm. It's like magic," says Diana, who averages 70 paintings a year, requiring the ink of four octopus.

"There are lots of octopus in Halibut Cove. It doesn't kill them to take the ink. But the terrible truth is . . ." says Diana, laughing, "we eat them anyway. They're very tasty."

Diana first came to Alaska when she was a little girl. She went to Homer High School. Homer was a tiny town then, with no dock and only about 12 fishing boats. Today, the harbor is filled with more than 400 fishing and recreational boats. Diana saw Halibut Cove for the first time on "senior sneak" when there were just a few old Norwegian fishermen living around the shore.

Meanwhile, Clem was back in

At low tide, Diana Tillion carries back an octopus she has captured. "There are lots of octopus in Halibut Cove. It doesn't kill them to take the ink. But the terrible truth is . . . we eat them anyway. They're very tasty."
(Fran Durner, Anchorage Daily News)

New York, running away from home. "Childhood wasn't much fun," he says. "Somebody was always telling me what to do."

So at age 18, he was in the South Pacific sitting under a coconut tree . . . in a foxhole. He was in the Seabees. It was during an air raid over the Solomon Islands in 1944. He had persistent tropical diseases, malaria and fungus growth. The doctor said he was a mess. His foxhole buddy suggested Clem go to Alaska. He could shake his dis-

*"The ocean is so powerful and unyielding. You cannot help but be dazzled by it. I use octopus ink to paint things of great intensity. To me, it's a living color, a gift from the sea."*

*—Diana*

eases better in a cold climate and cash in on the free land the U.S. government was giving away to people who would homestead. There in the malaria-infested tropics, the idea took root.

Clem was shipped back to San Francisco, where he went AWOL (Absent Without Leave). The military calls it desertion. Clem says, "I was going home to New York. I had no intention of deserting. I hadn't been home in a while." He grins.

"Now Clem, tell the truth," orders Diana.

"Well, you see, there was this little girl on the bus to Las Cruces, New Mexico," begins Clem with a kind of sheepish delight. "I had drawn a year's pay. I knew nothing about girls. They literally terrified me. I wanted to learn something about them. I thought, *'That* looks *niiice!'* They didn't have any of that out in the jungle.

"When they picked me up 40 days later, I didn't have any money. And I hadn't drunk a drop of liquor. But I had invested my year's pay very well. They did everything but court-martial me."

In 1946, Clem was finally discharged and headed for Alaska. He got to Anchorage, then jumped the train south for Moose Pass, walked from there

about 70 miles to the Kenai River and rafted down to the coast.

"I thought I was below the rapids, but I wasn't. It was kind of thrilling," says the red-haired fisherman with a gleam of those wild lights in his eyes. "From there, I walked down the beach to Kasilof, up the Kasilof River, around Tustumena Lake, and down the Fox River into Homer and found *her,*" he grins over at Diana.

Diana remembers, "I was picking berries when I heard these two fellows coming out of the woods. One of them was screaming, just screaming in a high-pitched angry voice. I thought if this guy sees me, he's going to be very embarrassed. So I went up to the porch of the house. His friend saw me. He egged Clem on to an even higher-pitched squeal. When they got right up to me, his friend tapped him on the shoulder. Clem turned and saw me. His mouth clamped shut and he turned purple and down the road they went. I didn't know that was Clem until a year after we were married.

"I was once again picking raspberries right out here in the garden at Halibut Cove. Clem had gone to the coal beach for a load of coal. When I married Clem, he never said a swear word or used any indecent language at all. Anyway, he came into the cove with a skiff load of coal, just smoking. I could see the skiff had taken a wave and was sinking. As long as he kept going, you see, it wouldn't sink. He was trying to get it close enough to the beach to dry dock it. So he came tearing in. He leapt out of the boat and tried to untie the line before the boat sank, but it was too tight. He just exploded with this voice, squealing at the top of his lungs.

"I thought to myself with horror, 'That's *that* man!' So I ducked down behind the raspberry bushes. I asked him when he came ashore, 'Did you know it was *me* on that porch?'"

Clem says jokingly, "When I first saw Diana, I fell so hard I was picking splinters out of my nose. All the bricks were stacked in the most appealing way." He beams. "But there was more than that. There's never been anybody else who's wowed me out like that. And you know what? When you're in love, it never gets old. When I go out even for a day, I get excited to come home. Isn't that what fairy tales are all about? And they lived happily in utter chaos ever after . . ."

Clem proposed to Diana on their first date. He'd invited her down to the docks to watch him pull halibut gear. He remembers, "I couldn't talk in front of her. I kept choking. I had trouble swallowing. I could only stare."

"At first, I thought he was rather homely," laughs Diana. "After all, he was 135 pounds and bright yellow from the malaria. But he was so jolly and never self-conscious, except of course around me. As soon as he started courting me, he began gulping and turning red. He picked up this terrible anxiety."

In the end, that's what made her fall for him. Everything else about him was "so organized and calculated," she remembers.

They married in November 1948.

Sitting in the solarium of their large rambling house, watching the midnight sun glow pink on the mountains and the tide wash into the cove, Diana and Clem remember those early years on their little island when they had only a few bachelor neighbors and were living a near-subsistence life.

"No woman can truly live in the wilderness if she doesn't have some old bachelors who come over for a cup of coffee and some home cooking—fellows who actually pick up the pieces while her husband is madly charging off into the hills after

*"So many homesteaders' and fishermen's wives were unhappy. You could just watch them get old and ground down. I don't know what the difference was. Probably, they weren't both sharing in the dream. Everything Diana had was just as rough. They took some of those women out of here in straitjackets. The ones who succeeded were the ones who went right on the boat with their husbands so they were an active part of it."*

*—Clem*

Left: *"I can easily paint a painting with one drop of octopus ink. It's so incredibly dense and warm,"* says Diana in her studio. (Fran Durner, Anchorage Daily News)
Below: *A Tillion octopus-ink painting of southeast Alaska spirits and Shamen.* (Anchorage Times)

*The shrimp plant, a painting by Diana Tillion.* (Anchorage Times)

whatever," says Clem. "Little things always happen the day you leave, like the roof blows off the house or the boat engine won't start and your wife is stranded. Women's lib might make it in the city, but neither men's lib nor women's lib make it in the bush."

"My mother must have been terribly anxious," says Diana. "But I wasn't. I was in love. I was having babies. We were doing things. We started a shrimp plant that went belly up, but we didn't know it was going to go belly up so we were as happy as can be working our tails off. I washed clothes on a scrub board outdoors. There was no sink. We only had an out-house. But you don't have time to think about how rough it is."

Adds Clem: "So many homesteaders' and fishermen's wives were unhappy. You could just watch them get old and ground down. I don't know what the difference was. Probably, they weren't both sharing in the dream. Everything Diana had was just as rough. They took some of those women out of here in straitjackets. The ones who succeeded were the ones who went right on the boat with their husbands so they were an active part of it. Then it's not 'my husband's boat,' it's 'our boat.' Then they could hack it."

Diana agrees. "I think being an artist made the difference. As soon as I could, I went out and fished and got money to build myself a studio. So I had my own little world which I still have and which I think every woman ought to have."

A few Christmases ago, she wrote and illustrated a book of stories about her four children growing up in Halibut Cove. They are all grown now with homes of their own in the cove.

Will, 41, has his captain's license for tugboats and 100-ton ships. In the winter, he long-lines for cod out in the wild waters of the Gulf of Alaska. When the storms roll in, the seas can sometimes get to 60 feet, and as Clem says, "There's no place to hide."

*Marian Tillion Beck welcomes Hector to the Halibut Cove dock. Marian has raised many orphaned seal pups in the Cove.* (Fran Durner, Anchorage Daily News)

Marian, the second oldest, 36, lives at the end of the boardwalk on the other side of the island. She owns and captains the ferry between Homer and the cove, fishes salmon in Cook Inlet, and runs a little sushi restaurant in the cove called "The Saltry." She raises abandoned seal pups and, like her mother, she is also an artist.

Martha, 32, is a doctor. She is married to one of Alaska's state legislators, Sam Cotten, and to-gether they have a home on the far shore of the cove.

Vincent, the youngest at 29, has his 500-ton captain's license and skippers ships through the Panama Canal to the North Pacific.

Like their father, says Diana, at least three of her four children are adrenaline addicts. And when four out of six in the family are captains, things can get wild.

"Marian and I strike sparks,"

*"As a politician, don't ever make me decide between the fish and the fishermen. Because I'll always decide for the fish. That's what this country will live on for the next 1,000 years. That's why I was in the legislature—so my grandson will have some fish to fish. And I want his grandson to have a future too."*

*—Clem*

says Clem. "When we're on the boat together, we know it's explosive so we walk a fine line. One is usually in charge. The first thing you have to settle is who's boss."

Diana adds: "The older Clem gets, the more often Marian is in charge. I used to have a photograph of them, the profiles, nose to nose, with the identical expression. They were having some sort of explosive tiff."

Both Clem and Diana laugh about the memory of it all.

Not only are they proud parents, but they are also, as Clem says, "Damn well proud to have some Alaskans in the family." To the red-haired patriarch, "An Alaskan is one who was born here and is going to be buried here. Anybody else is just a snowbird."

In 1962, Clem received a telegram: "Congratulations! You're running for the state legislature."

The incumbent legislator had filed Clem's name instead of his own. So the Halibut Cove fisherman donned a new hat—a black bowler derby—and went on the campaign trail. Together with his red hair, red suspenders, and strong opinions, he was not easily forgettable, which was exactly what he intended. Elected in 1962, he served for 18 colorful and controversial years, end-

ing up his term as president of the Alaska State Senate.

"Being a politician is like being a lawyer," Clem observes. "It's possible to serve with honor, but not easy. You can play every trick and every game, but in the end, are you true unto that which you went to serve?"

Politics and fish is an explosive combination in this far northern state, a combination that makes Clem's juices flow. In defense of fish, he's got plenty of fingers in the political stew. He has been an adviser to the president of the United States on oceans and atmosphere. For many years, he served on and chaired the North Pacific Fisheries Management Council, one of six regional councils in the country responsible for allocating the fishery resources within the United States' 200-mile limit. He still serves as a U.S. member, presidentially appointed, on the International North Pacific Fisheries Commission.

"As a politician, don't ever make me decide between the fish and the fishermen. Because I'll always decide for the fish. That's what this country will live on for the next 1,000 years. That's why I was in the legislature—so my grandson will have some fish to fish. And I want his grandson to have a future too."

A large percentage of Alaska's fish goes to Japan every year. For many years, on behalf of Alaska and the U.S. government, Clem Tillion has been a negotiator in the international fisheries arena.

"The Japanese have an absolutely predatory outlook on our fish, while a very protective outlook on their fisheries. I don't feel any differently. I might with a plundering army totally lay waste another man's land, while fight to the death to protect my own. So I understand that. I don't expect them to have a conservation ethic in mind. But I'll brutally make sure they do or else. I haven't been soft with them."

Diana adds: "The Japanese have a lot of respect for Clem. They say 'Mr. Tillion is never kind, but he is honest. When he says no, he's sorry, but we know he means that.'"

"The thing I can't understand, says Clem, "is these liberals who say: 'Throw them out. Crack down on those multinationals.'

"I say, 'Hey, have you ever been to northern Hokkaido in Japan and seen those bent little old ladies mending their nets in the snow on the dock? That's who you're looking at. And while I'm willing to take the fish away from them, I will do it

*"My love for this place is kind of like our marriage. Somebody once asked my wife, 'Have you ever considered divorce?' Diana looked startled for a moment and then said, 'No. Murder, yes. But not divorce.'" Clem grins. "It's the same with this country. I get so exasperated with it sometimes, but the thought of living anywhere else—no way."*

only if there is an American fisherman ready to harvest them.

"As my grandfather, who was a mercenary, said, 'Never inflict pain without profit. That's sadism.' And these people who would kick the Japanese out before we're ready to take over the fishery are sadists. I will not do that. I squeezed them constantly. I made no bones about where my goal was. But I needed that pressure to force my own country to develop its fisheries."

In 1980, after Clem's retirement from state politics, former governor Jay Hammond came to Halibut Cove to encourage Clem to run for governor.

"I said no. Why? Because it's the end of my life. I'd have to give up this." He gestures with a wide sweeping motion towards

Clem Tillion chairs an international fisheries meeting between the United States and Japan, 1983. (Paul Brown, Anchorage Daily News)

all that lies outside the windows of the solarium. It is one of those golden, jewel-like evenings where the water sparkles, an eagle swoops low over the trees, the mountains are breathtaking, and the smell of saltwater and freedom is heavy in the breeze. "I could never have it back. I paid my dues. I did my time.

"You know, when I first came along this coast, I was looking for a place where I could raise a family and not worry about feeding them; a place where I could protect what I had. This was it. I fell in love with Kachemak Bay.

"My love for this place is kind of like our marriage. Somebody once asked my wife, 'Have you ever considered divorce?'

"Diana looked startled for a moment and then said, 'No. Murder, yes. But not divorce.'" Clem laughs jovially with a mischievous grin across the room at Diana.

"It's the same with this country. I get so exasperated with it sometimes, but the thought of living anywhere else—no way. Unless I drown and they never find my body, I'll be buried here."

# 15

# The Camp Fire Girls

eeeeyyy, Camp Fire . . ."
The words were magic and spoken low with a kind of reverence. Little Eskimo children kicked through the mud in their knee-high boots, their fingers and faces stained blue from berry picking.

Entertainment had come to town.

The plane touched down outside the log cabin terminal in Bethel, an Eskimo community on the banks of the Kuskokwim River in southwest Alaska. It was the summer of 1971. Half a dozen starry-eyed college girls, most of whom had never stepped foot in Alaska before, descended from the plane, packs slung over their backs. With the confidence of those who think they have the world by its tail, they swung into the back of a pickup truck for the ride into town.

There were only six miles of road, stretching from the dirt runway of the airstrip over the rolling treeless tundra. On the way they passed a large billboard announc-

*Carroll Hodge (left) and Sally Mead gather around a campfire at Kenai Lake on a stormy summer morning in 1987. It was here 16 years ago that they began their careers in Alaska as counselors for Camp Fire Girls. They traveled around Alaska teaching swimming in Indian and Eskimo villages. (Nan Elliot)*

ing: "Welcome. You are now entering the Bethel National Forest." Behind it stood one lone, sickly, transplanted swamp spruce tree about four feet tall. Twenty yards down the road another huge billboard announced: "Thank you. You are now leaving the Bethel National Forest."

The young women drew a crowd of little admirers. It was the end of the summer. Children were back from fish camp. Their dark, shy faces were stuffed with snuff. They followed their new swimming instructors everywhere.

"Heeeeyyy, Camp Fire . . ." they sang out in their soft, melodic voices, ". . . we go swim now?"

Beginning in the 1960s, Camp Fire Girls of Alaska had an innovative wilderness adventure camp on the Kenai Lake, 100 miles south of Anchorage. From there, the director sent teams of counselors out every summer on swimming projects in Indian and Eskimo villages.

Alaska leads the nation in the number of drowning deaths per capita. Commercial fishing is one of its largest industries and subsistence fishing is a way of life for many rural and Native people. Most Alaskans live and work around the water, but 20

*Carroll Hodge, filmmaker, at Kachemak Bay, 1988.* (Nan Elliot)

*There were no swimming pools. Instead they taught in rain-filled gravel pits, in sloughs, in the swift-moving waters of the Yukon River, or in a back eddy along the banks of the Kuskokwim. They were naive, idealistic, energetic, and filled with purpose. And many fell in love with Alaska.*

years ago few knew how to swim. Arctic weather is hardly enticing for jumping into oceans, rivers, or glacier-fed lakes, which are rarely above 45 degrees Fahrenheit on the warmest of days.

But here came the Camp Fire Girls, most of them from California, who were merrily teaching little kids to jump into water that no sane Alaskan would ever step foot in.

In those days, counselors were all young women. They taught in bush communities mainly in southcentral and southwest Alaska. There were no swimming pools. Instead they taught in rain-filled gravel pits, in sloughs, in the swift-moving waters of the Yukon River, or in a back eddy along the banks of the Kuskokwim. They were naive, idealistic, energetic, and filled with purpose. And many fell in love with Alaska.

Two of those were Carroll Hodge and Sally Mead, both from the golden shores of southern California.

"I remember going to Eskimo dancing in the quonset hut in Bethel. The drums were beating. Old men and women got up to dance. They acted out their stories and legends. They were funny. They were moving. They were poignant. You could feel the power of that storytelling tra-

dition, symbolic of Mother Earth herself. The whole culture at that moment for me was very alive," says Carroll Hodge. Her clear light blue eyes are intense and lively.

Those impressionable images of Native peoples during Camp Fire days were the beginnings of Carroll's career as a filmmaker. Now she is 41 years old, having just completed two major film projects. One is about an Eskimo family buried beneath a wave of ice at the edge of the Arctic Ocean and frozen in time for five centuries before being discovered. The second is a series of films on the history, drama, and questions surrounding one of the most significant political movements of our century—the settlement of Alaska Native Land Claims.

Sally Mead's first memory of Alaska was from the plane flying up from California for the first of her four summers as a Camp Fire counselor.

"It was a clear, sunny, summer day. Below me were mountains and mountains and mountains. The snow was . . . endless. It was the middle of June. I sat at the window awestruck. I felt like I was home for the first time in my life. Perhaps it was some sense of reincarnation, as if parts of my soul were here already."

Carroll and Sally are old friends, their bonds extending back to college in southern California. From their first summer in Alaska, Carroll reflects, "I think we both wondered why it took us so long to find this place."

Sally is remembered at camp as the all-American girl, bubbling with enthusiasm. Tall, with long brown hair and wire-rim glasses, she strode down the beach of Kenai Lake to the evening camp fire circle, her guitar in hand, followed by adoring campers.

Carroll was quiet, thoughtful, and committed to issues. "She had tons of energy and could be very funny," says Sally. "But mostly she was serious. She was a practicing Quaker then. It was a time she was considering getting U.S. citizenship. (Carroll was born in Montreal, Canada.) She went into the courthouse in Los Angeles for the formal ceremony, but when it came to the part about 'the right to bear arms' she got very emotional and walked out without finishing. Carroll didn't have the same conquest attitude that the rest of us did. She was always willing to climb up the mountain with you, but she didn't care if she got to the top. She always commanded tremendous respect, in large part for how she lived her daily life.

Carroll was all those things someone would want to admire."

While Carroll was in Oregon teaching in a ghetto school for two years, Sally was building onto a little cabin she had found in the woods, 20 minutes from downtown Anchorage. When Carroll returned, she moved into a tiny cabin down the road from Sally and began living what she happily describes as "the timber hippie" existence.

They chopped wood, hauled water, heated in barrel stoves, built camp fires in their backyards, ate "dumpster dinners" by scavenging edible throwaways outside grocery stores, and visited "city" friends for showers. They lived on a little dirt road named Dogwood Lane, later renamed "DeHart" by the city. To christen it, their friends hung an addition onto the street sign so it read: "DeHart of De Woods."

"What I loved immediately about Alaska was the spirit of the place . . . the sense that you cannot control this environment. You must be respectful of the land. That doesn't exist very many places," says Sally. "In California, there's nothing that draws you to the land. Even here in Anchorage, you can very easily stay in a nice warm house and drive a warm car, and you

*"What I loved immediately about Alaska was the spirit of the place . . . the sense that you cannot control this environment. You must be respectful of the land. That doesn't exist very many places," says Sally.*

*"I learned to fly because I'm probably too impatient to climb a mountain,"* says Sally, shown here with her dog, Harvest, at her cabin in Anchorage in 1978. *(Nan Elliot)*

don't have to deal with the elements. But to be out there in the woods puts us in our proper places. We aren't the controlling factor in the universe. There are a lot more powerful forces.

"When people band together in one little place called a city, they feel more powerful than the environment. Then they have this image that they can control, and consequently they destroy, pollute, and ruin the land."

Today Sally still lives in the woods with her two children in a huge log house she built herself on a narrow strip of land between the mountains and the sea about 40 minutes drive south of Anchorage. At their back door are thousands of acres of national forest and park lands.

Ever gracious, Sally Mead has a multidimensional, engaging personality. Today, she is the special assistant to the Alaska Commissioner of Health and Social Services. In the early days,

as a folk singer, she started a coffee house and became a kind of local folk star. She organized day care centers, worked as a counselor in mental health clinics, set up family and children's services for Native organizations in rural Alaska, and apprenticed herself to the well-known log cabin builder, Jimmy Hitchcock, so she could learn the trade and build her own house.

Physically strong and independent, she's as comfortable sitting behind the controls of a small airplane as she is wielding an axe and hammer.

"I learned to fly because I'm probably too impatient to climb a mountain . . . and maybe it's a little less strenuous." She smiles. "But you can have the same kind of challenges of life and death in an airplane. I was terrified at first. But once you get up there, it's open sky. All you have to do is pick your direction."

That's one thing Alaskans seem to have in common—a tremendous need for space. Visual, personal, and living space.

"Somehow, you have more freedom in Alaska," explains Carroll. "When I lived in Oregon, people always wanted to pass laws to control their neighbors or get their neighbors to think like they did. They were looking for homogeneity. In California, there was an urge to be different, to be weird, to stand out because you were already so much a part of the crowd. But up here, the attitude is 'just let me be.' And that brings out really different things in people. I wonder if people in Los Angeles sit around and talk about what it means to live in Los Angeles?"

Today, Carroll calls herself "a temporary exile," since her work in film takes her back and forth

*Carroll, director of a television series on the fisheries of Alaska, records sound on location at King Salmon, 1982. (Nan Elliot)*

*Carroll Hodge, director, and Ron Eagle, cameraman, film salmon in the Naknek River near Bristol Bay, 1982. A distinguished Alaska cinematographer, Ron Eagle died in 1988 while filming a white water rafting adventure for a program hosted by former Alaska governor Jay Hammond.* (Nan Elliot)

*"This place is so much more extreme than anywhere else I've ever been—higher, deeper, colder, lighter longer. And yet, instead of making you feel insignificant, it encourages you to be more of who you are."*

*—Carroll Hodge*

There's probably nobody else around who knows anything more than you do about this job, so go do it. That is very freeing. I felt in an absolutely different dimension. This place is so awesome, so much more extreme than anywhere else I've ever been—higher, deeper, colder, lighter longer. And yet, instead of making you feel like an insignificant puny person, it encourages you to be more of who you are."

With energy, imagination, and excitement towards her work, Carroll rose to the top of her profession in television in five years. So she went to Los Angeles to get a master's degree in film at the University of Southern California.

"At film school, it wasn't that I was any brighter, more creative, or a better filmmaker than others, but I was better at taking risks. If you survive a winter in Alaska out in the woods and come through some potentially risky times OK that means you aren't so intimidated the next time. It's the physical side of life up here that makes a difference."

Interestingly enough, in their own different arenas, both Carroll, through film, and Sally, through her work in mental health, have become intensely

between Alaska and Hollywood. Shortly after Carroll arrived back in Alaska during the timber-hippie cabin-in-the-woods era of her life, she went to work for the public television station when it first went on the air as a writer/producer/host for a series of shows on local issues and personalities.

"If my first job had been in New York or Los Angeles, I would have been competing like a maniac for what I was doing. That's such a different approach to work than realizing there's nobody nipping at your heels.

involved in the lives and cultures of the Native peoples of Alaska.

"I think there's a romantic notion among white folks that they want Native people to preserve their traditional, ancient ways. While that's very unfair to expect them to be a museum for us, I can understand the impulse," says Carroll. "They were the original conservationists, living in harmony with the earth. As our world gets more corrupted and polluted, we need to keep in touch with those who have a knowledge of the old ways. Maybe these people who truly live off the land know something we don't know and we can tap into their spiritualness. In order to save the planet, we need people who are that connected to the earth.

"In many ways, I identify with their values. Harmony versus confrontation. Enjoying the beauty of the land versus the ownership of the land. That's important. Almost like breathing. The differences I find intrinsically fascinating—their legends, their stories, their religion, and their unique sense of humor. The differences made it interesting to be involved in their culture and the likenesses I felt made it comfortable."

"The Frozen Family of Utqiagvik" was a film Carroll

Trekking through the Himalayas in 1980, Sally stops at one of the local Nepalese tea houses for her daily ration of Lemu sodas. A pilot and a log cabin builder, Sally is also a mental health therapist and today works all over Alaska as special assistant to the governor's commissioner of Health and Social Services. (Nan Elliot)

*"Why should they listen to me? They have every reason to hate me for it is my culture, the white culture, that has created so many problems for them—beginning with the Russian fur traders who enslaved the Aleuts to hunt sea otters for them 200 years ago. But maybe some of the skills I have, if I'm careful not to impose, can give them the tools they need right now to help themselves."*

*—Sally*

wrote and produced for public television in Alaska in 1986. Utqiagvik is the old name for Barrow, an Eskimo whaling community on the coast of the Arctic Ocean, the farthest north town in America. Five hundred years ago, a wave of ice crashed over the bluff during a storm and buried a small sod and timber house under tons of ice. The women and children inside died instantly. For five centuries they were frozen in ice. But every year the Arctic Ocean and weather were wearing away the bluff and exposing more of the past.

In 1982, two young people from Barrow searching for old artifacts along the bluff found a foot, then another foot connected to a leg. They notified the police. Eskimo people thought they were recent burials, murders never reported.

"The bodies were so well preserved, they still had body fluids in them," says Carroll. "A lot of significant medical information was learned. The women had black lungs because they were the ones who slept near and tended the seal oil lamp. The bones, when x-rayed, showed tiny cracks, a slowing of growth

due to malnutrition. No matter how much food was gathered the year before, there was always a lean period every spring before the snows thawed. Piecing together the story of the family was fascinating. You can imagine, the anthropologists went wild.

"I am drawn to these different Native cultures in Alaska because they are so strong, and they are of this place, and they are going through so much change," says Carroll. "It's interesting to look at how human beings adapt. I come from a family of six. I like the idea of doing things by consensus. I like the idea of village Alaska—how people learn about the land around them, how they share, how they can include so many in their extended families. Those are the good parts of who I am."

While Carroll, as the observer, approaches her work from the outside looking in, Sally, as a mental health therapist, attempts to get on the inside to expand the vision outward.

"Native cultures in Alaska—Aleut, Indian, Eskimo—are all having problems of destruction: identity crises, alcoholism, family disintegration," says Sally.

"Why should they listen to me? They have every reason to hate me for it is my culture, the white culture, that has created so many problems for them—beginning with the Russian fur traders who enslaved the Aleuts to hunt sea otters for them 200 years ago. But maybe some of the skills I have, if I'm careful not to impose, can give them the tools they need right now to help themselves."

Sally spent five years developing a program for the Chugach Native Association to provide services for family and children in villages and communities in the Kachemak Bay-Prince William Sound region of southcentral Alaska. The region is a mixture of overlapping Aleut, Indian, and Eskimo cultures. Sally would travel from village to village, talking, learning, forging strong, sometimes stormy, bonds with people, always searching and struggling with them to find a key to solve community problems. It wasn't easy to be accepted.

"Let me give you an example of why you have to look at the whole history of social patterns in a community, not just isolate something like alcoholism and try and treat that. I don't want to be too harsh on Christianity, but a great number of difficulties arose when Christian religions were introduced in Alaska. They had a lot to do with the breaking down of rituals which are important to people.

"In Aleut culture there is a fascinating ritual called 'trance dancing.' People would get into a kind of hypnotic trance and dance out their evil.

"Well of course, the Christian church came and forbid that to be done. People were told to go to confessional instead. But it doesn't work the same way and besides, it wasn't their ritual. So what happened is that the Aleuts started acting out their evil rather than releasing it. You

*Therapy is done around the breakfast table, in a boat going down the bay, on a log by the beach. "I'm not the kind of person who wants to dress in high heel shoes and see upper middle-class people in an office all day. There's something so confining about it. First of all, you can't walk around in those kind of shoes."*

*Carroll, Sally, and Sally's daughter, Cloé, camping at Kenai Lake, 1987.*
(Nan Elliot)

bring alcohol into the picture and destructive, horrible things happen. A counseling program for the alcoholic then is totally irrelevant. You're not getting anywhere near the root of the problem.

"The only way the system will heal is if it heals from within and creates its own meaning. They've got to decide what works from the past and what they've learned today and out of that develop their own set of rituals. The way I've seen that work with psychotherapy in one village is that we were able to get the couple with the most severe problems to a point where they could see health. Then it was just a matter of supporting their movement forward. And

everything started to happen on its own.

"The man, an alcoholic for 20 years, became a healer, a new modern-day healer in the village. The woman, who once told me, 'I'm half white and I'm half Native and it's very lonely here,' started an Alcoholics Anonymous group with this man. Slowly, people in the village started coming because they were curious to see how this man got healthy. Like a yeast, it started growing from the inside out. This man, who is becoming the village healer, may preach things that he's learned, but he doesn't have anyone telling him how to do his healing. He's making it up as he goes along in response to all the people there. And that to me is the key."

One of the wonderful parts of traveling to the villages for Sally is that therapy is done around the breakfast table, in a boat going down the bay, on a log by the beach.

"I'm not the kind of person who wants to dress in high heel shoes and see upper middle-class people in an office every day. There's something so confining about it. First of all, you can't walk around in those kind of shoes."

Even feet need space in Alaska.

# 16

# Last Of The Arctic Whalemen

A gallant gentleman of 84, Ted Pedersen was once a cabin boy on the last steam whaler in the Arctic. Only a man with Viking and Aleut blood in his veins could have lived the life Captain Pedersen has lived. And survived.

In 1919, as a small boy at sea, he was in a slender, wooden boat, chasing a bowhead whale in the Arctic Ocean. All of a sudden, that leviathan of the deep rose out of the water like a mountain of vengeance and flipped the tiny whaleboat and all of its crew into the ice-choked sea. Teddy did not know how to swim. To make matters worse, he was trapped under the boat.

Since then, he's been washed out of his bunk and washed overboard several times. In these frigid northern waters, it's a miracle he's alive today.

As a young man, after many years at sea, Ted joined the Lighthouse Service. He was keeper of the farthest west lighthouse in America on Unimak Island, one of the

*The* Olga *in stormy seas: In 1903, Ted Pedersen's father, the famous Norwegian "Ice Pilot," Captain C.T. Pedersen, was sailing the Arctic Ocean as mate on the small sailing schooner* Olga. *(University of Alaska Fairbanks)*
Inset: *Ted Pedersen in 1988, skipper of the* White Whale. *(Nan Elliot)*

Aleutian Islands, which stretch a thousand miles from Alaska towards the heart of Siberia. The northern link in the Pacific "ring of fire," the Aleutians are volcanic islands still spewing forth smoke, fire, and ash. It is here that the warm waters of the Pacific Ocean meet the cold waters of the Bering Sea.

Storms are violent. Earthquakes rumble beneath the ocean floor. It is a cauldron of natural disasters. It is also a treeless chain of islands of extraordinary beauty, the ancestral home of the Aleut people, Ted's people. Unimak Island was named "The Roof of Hell" by the first Russian fur traders who saw it more than 200 years ago. It is built of smoking volcanoes, still active.

"My front yard was the Bering Sea and in my backyard were four volcanoes and the Pacific Ocean," says Teddy. "It's one of the foggiest and stormiest places in the world. Sailors called that place 'the graveyard of the Pacific.'"

The lighthouse served to guide ships through the pass—Unimak Pass—between two islands and between the two seas. Wreckage littered the reefs, a testimony to the courage and sorrow of navigating in some of the most dangerous waters in the world. During Ted's six years

*A gallant gentleman of 84, Ted Pedersen was once a cabin boy on the last steam whaler in the Arctic. Only a man with Viking and Aleut blood in his veins could have lived the life Captain Pedersen has lived. And survived.*

out at Cape Sarichef on Unimak Island, he risked his life several times to row into turbulent seas, ferrying shipwrecked survivors between boats and shore.

About 10 years after he left the Lighthouse Service and was living at his homestead in Bear Cove, Ted was down on the beach digging clams. It was 1946. The neighboring fox farmer's wife rowed over with the news. The lighthouse at Scotch Cap, 20 miles across Unimak Island from Cape Sarichef and facing the Pacific Ocean, had been completely demolished by a 100-foot tidal wave. All five men perished.

When he was 59 years old, Ted was a seaman aboard an oil tanker in Resurrection Bay. Ten minutes before the largest earthquake in the history of North America devastated the face of Alaska on March 27, 1964, he had just stepped off the ship onto the dock at Seward to relieve the sailor handling the

*"This photo was taken on the* Herman *returning from the Arctic in 1921. This is the nurse who captured my dad's fancy. She also convinced Dad to send me to Mount Hermon School. May I one day prove it was worthwhile by writing my yarn of the old days in the Arctic." Left to right: Ted, the nurse his dad married, and Captain Pedersen. (Pedersen Collection)*

valves pumping gas and oil into the ship's hold.

At 5:36 p.m, "all hell broke loose."

The dock where Teddy was standing began to pitch and roll. All the pilings pulled up. The tanker was violently slamming into the dock. The fuel lines ripped apart and oil and gas began spewing into the air. Ted tried to run to shore, but saw he would never make it. So he turned back for the tanker. The dock collapsed into splinters. The

ocean and port were ablaze with fire. Teddy jumped from one fragment of disintegrating dock to another like they were ice floes bobbing on the ocean. His footing gave way and he fell into the water.

As he looked up, "a wave loaded with timber" came crashing down upon his head. He closed his eyes and waited for the end.

The next thing he knew, he was stomach down on the catwalk of the tanker, miraculously

*"I was 11 when I went to sea. This was my first day on the ship. See this tie I had on? I didn't take that tie off for 27 days. That's how long it took us to get from the Aleutians to San Francisco."* (Pedersen Collection)

flung out of the water by the violence of the pounding waves and tossed back up on the ship. Both his legs were broken. He was "black, blue, and green." But he was alive.

The crew managed to get the ship out into the bay to ride out the waves. The ship's pilot later told Ted, "One more minute near shore and the whole ship would have exploded. The sides were heavily blistered from the fire."

The Great Alaska Earthquake of 1964 measured 8.6 on the Richter scale. The tremors and waves were felt from Alaska to Antarctica. Whole towns and villages at the edge of the sea were destroyed by the violent waves. The greatest death came from the sea. Ninety-two people were drowned or swept away. Most bodies were never recovered. Ted was one of the lucky ones.

When he was 80 years old, Ted finally retired from piloting cargo ships and tankers through Alaska waters. He had big plans. He wanted to finish the *White Whale*, a perfect replica of the old New Bedford whaleboat that nearly tossed him to Davy Jones in 1919. He named it after Moby Dick.

"But you know," he says sadly, "no one remembers the White Whale anymore. And they think a whaleboat is one of those plastic things with a motor on it they call a Boston whaler."

*"I was off watch in my bunk. It was cold, so I had my socks and underwear on and just my outer clothes off. All of a sudden, I heard the ship. She was riding the swell. What happened was the captain took the ship over that northeast bar going into Kodiak. The water was shallow there so the waves built up. The boat rode those swells. She'd come up and then she'd run down those swells. And then she broached. She went on her side."*

Only five other models of Teddy's whaleboat exist in America today, he says. All are in museums. Ted started building his boat and with the help of the Nordic Boat Shop in Seattle, he finished it. In the spring of 1986, on the mud flats of Ship Creek in Anchorage, Captain Pedersen pushed his little craft into the rough waters of Cook Inlet, unfurled the white sail with the great sperm whale on top, and stood at the rudder, sailing south for 200 miles into his homestead at Bear Cove.

Despite his age, Ted is still as strong as an ox. His voice is deep and booming. He loves telling the story of a middle-aged British couple who were having breakfast near his table a few years ago at a little cafe in New Zealand where he went one winter to escape the cold.

"The fellow sat down at the table and said to his wife, 'I say, love, crack me a couple of jolly eggs. I feel beastly active today.'" Ted grins a mischievous grin and says, "I'm 84 years old and beastly active myself."

Part Aleut and part Norwegian, Ted is a handsome man with swarthy skin, wispy white hair, and twinkling eyes. Although he has lived alone for more than 17 years in a remote and beautiful place in Alaska, accessible only by plane or boat, the old sailor is a gentleman in all the best senses of the word. Bear Cove has been his home for 40 years. He has built two homesteads there and is now clearing the land to build himself a third one, a smaller one, on the island in the cove where he can look out at his beloved mountaintop glaciers and write his many yarns. He has a thousand stories to tell and what transpires briefly on these pages is merely, as they say, the tip of the iceberg.

"The worst storm I've been in? I don't know. I've been scared so many times.

"On the mail boat once I was washed out of my bunk. I was mate. It was January. From Seward, we were headed for Kodiak.

We went through the pass there. It was snowing. The skipper decided to anchor. He should have gone into a little more shelter. But there was a swell running. We had a 2,500-pound anchor and that just parted the chain. We dropped the other anchor. That parted too. So we lost both anchors. The captain decided he'd make a run for it into Kodiak. Well, that's impossible when you have a heavy swell. Radar is useless. It's all white spots. You can't pick up the buoys. So he headed for the channel.

"I was off watch in my bunk. It was cold, so I had my socks and underwear on and just my outer clothes off. All of a sudden, I heard the ship. She was riding the swell. What happened was the captain took the ship over that northeast bar going into Kodiak. The water was shallow there so the waves built up. The boat rode those swells. She'd come up and then she'd run down those swells. And then she broached. She went on her side.

"When the rudder's out of the water and you're riding down the swell, there's no control over it. The propeller's just spinning. I heard this.

"Then all of a sudden, we're laying on our side. The water just poured into my room. I

*Ted's father, Captain Christian Theodore Pedersen, was born in 1876 in Sandefjord, Norway. (Pedersen Collection)*

jumped out of my bunk. Life preservers from the passengers' quarters were floating by me. I grabbed a couple and ran up to the pilot house in my underwear and socks.

"The engineer hollered up: 'Tell the captain we can't take any more like that.'

"If we had had any deck load at all, we would have just stayed over on one side. Fortunately, the boat came back up. During the war, a ship did the same thing there and they lost all hands. There must have been about 30 or 40 men on board. They just got into the swell and she broached and rolled over.

"In that situation, you've got

Ted Pedersen has an exotic seafaring heritage. His maternal grandfather was Russian; his mother was Aleut, a people who for centuries were master mariners in their tiny skinboats; and his father was Norwegian, the internationally famous "Ice Pilot," Captain C.T. Pedersen, the last of the Arctic whalemen.

**Above**: *Ted's mother, sister, and himself as a baby. The photo was taken two weeks before his mother died in 1906.*
**Right**: *"That's my sister. She was a real flapper!"* (Pedersen Collection)

*Bear Cove, Kachemak Bay, 1950. (Pedersen Collection)*

to turn and run into the storm. Then, if there's a heavy swell, you're heading into it and you have oil bags you put out to keep the water from combing. You see, it's the combing that piles aboard. The breaking wave—that's where the power is. But if you put oil on it—they call it 'storm oil'—there won't be any whitecaps. On a sailing ship, you put the sail up to the windward, the wheel the other way, and the ship just lays into the weather. On each side, you have these big bags loaded with oakum and oil.

The oil just seeps out and puts a little slick on the water. I learned that from my father coming from San Francisco into the Aleutians every spring when we had a lot of heavy weather."

Ted loves telling stories. When two young women kayaked down the bay to hear them one summer, he rolled out one adventure after another.

After several hours, he got a sly look on his face and a mock frown, stood up, and said, "If you two scissorbills would stop talking, I could get some work

done." He has a million projects—clearing land, cutting trees, burning stumps, fixing boats, or building a sauna.

As the pastel colors of twilight glimmer off the water, he clambered into his boat and rowed out to pull up his crab and shrimp pots for dinner.

Ted's home is an old schoolhouse that he floated down the bay from the town of Seldovia. He built it up on pilings at the head of the cove and painted it bright red. Twice a day, the high tides of Kachemak Bay wash up

*"Time means something at my age. When I look out and see the water and the beauty of it all, I say, 'Thank God to be alive!' How many people have this kind of serenity and peace. I'm a free human being. No one gives me orders. I do as I please."*

beneath the house. There's a porthole off the kitchen and a spy glass to watch the weather. A ship's bell hangs over his bunk ringing the hour. Two bells and he's awake. For landlubbers, that's five o'clock in the morning.

"Time means something at my age," says Ted. "When I look out and see the water and the beauty of it all, I say, 'Thank God to be alive!' How many people have this kind of serenity and peace. I'm a free human being. No one gives me orders. I do as I please."

The original Pedersen homestead lies on the east side of the cove in a more pastoral setting of cleared grassy land and little cabins. But Ted left in 1971, heartbroken.

One day, he was out in the woods, clearing a field. He heard a shot. He listened carefully. Three shots in the woods means "danger." Two more shots and

he ran back to the cabin. He burst in.

"Elsa, what's wrong?" His wife of 30 years was a celebrated author of children's stories. All had been written at Bear Cove.

"'I'm fed up on Bear Cove,' she said. I told her to go to Homer and get a change of scenery. She radioed for the plane. I went into the woods. I didn't want to watch her go. I heard the plane come. Then it went away. She never came back. That's how it ended after 30 years. In 15 minutes. I went back to the cabin. In her typewriter was a note: 'I want no part of Bear Cove.' Only the year before I heard her say she'd like to have her bones buried in the cove with a tree growing over them."

Ted's eyes fill with tears, as they do every time he tells this story.

"She fell in love with my half brother, Walt. He had money, planes, and he was 10 years younger. I don't blame him. With all my trips to sea, I guess I went away too far and stayed away too long."

Ted Pedersen has an exotic seafaring heritage. His maternal grandfather was Russian; his mother was Aleut, a people who for centuries were master mariners in their tiny skin boats; and his father was Norwegian, the internationally famous "Ice Pilot," Captain Christian Theodore Pedersen, the last of the Arctic whalemen. In 1921, the last bowhead whale in the Arctic taken for commercial enterprise was harpooned and taken by Captain C.T. Pedersen's crew on the ship the *Herman*.

Born in 1905 on Samalga, a small island just off the tip of Umnak in the Aleutian Islands, Ted spent most of the first 11 years of his life in an orphanage 100 miles to the west in Dutch Harbor on the island of Unalaska.

His father had met his mother while sea otter hunting in the Aleutians. But she died in childbirth when Ted was only a year old.

"It used to bother me when I was a kid. They called me half-breed. I never knew my mother's name. When I got my marriage license, I had to ask my dad. I had never seen a picture of her. Not until five years ago. One of my cousins had it. I saw it and said, 'Now I belong to somebody,'" Ted says softly.

"My father never mentioned her. But my aunt told me my dad was very much in love with her. He was blonde and a six-footer. My mom was like a little doll. My dad would hold his

*After many years at sea, Ted joined the Lighthouse Service. One of his first postings was at Cape St. Elias, where he is shown here washing his clothes.* (Pedersen Collection)

*The lighthouse served to guide ships through the pass—Unimak Pass—between two islands and between the two seas. Wreckage littered the reefs, a testimony to the courage and sorrow of navigating in some of the most dangerous waters in the world.*

*At the end of Kachemak Bay in Bear Cove, Ted built his first homestead in the 1940s. (Pedersen Collection)*

arm out and she just fit underneath it.

"I never knew my dad until he took me out of the orphan home. But when he sailed through the Aleutians he would leave presents for me and a pail of candy for the home. The day he picked me up, a fellow came and gave me a little bag of sweets. Nobody told me where I was going. But they took me to the *Herman* and I knew my father was skipper. He was very well-known and well-liked. From 1894 to 1936, he made 40 trips to the Arctic. He lost only one ship that was crushed in the ice, the *Elvira*. They called him 'The Ice Pilot.'

"I came aboard. It really impressed me. The steam smoke stack and all those big cross-yards. I went below and the cook gave me a bowl of barley soup. It had about a quarter of an inch of grease on the top. I had a little bunk next to the porthole. And oh, I was really seasick. Water was splashing against the porthole and I kept asking the mate when we were going to anchor. See this tie I had on in this photo? That was my first day on the ship. I didn't take that tie off for 27 days. It took us that long to get to San Francisco.

"I slept down in the fo'c's'le

*"The crew and mates really respected my father. They didn't trust anyone else in the crow's nest when the ship was in ice except my dad. Sometimes, the ice would squeeze us in and we'd get ready to abandon ship. But the thing I remember most were the storms. Wow. Big combers coming in and breaking waves over the ship. It really felt good when we came out of them. I was so scared my knees were shaking."*

Above: *Captain C.T. Pedersen on the ship* Herman, *circa 1917.*
Left: *Ted as quartermaster. (Pedersen Collection)*

*The whaler,* Herman, *in the Arctic, circa 1916: "Every year, we made a round trip between San Francisco and the Arctic. All that territory we were trading. When we were through, we'd go after whales." (Pedersen Collection)*

with all the sailors. No one told me what to do. I just flopped down with all my clothes on. For three years, I was down there. When I finally got a room aft, my dad said, 'Teddy, I hope you don't think I was too hard on you, but that's where I got my start—down in the fo'c's'le.'

"My dad always called me 'Teddy.' He was hard on me. But I admired my dad.

"The crew and mates really respected my father. They didn't trust anyone else in the crow's nest when the ship was in ice except my dad. Sometimes, the ice would squeeze us in and we'd get ready to abandon ship. But the thing I remember most were the storms. Wow. Big combers coming in and breaking waves over the ship. It really felt good when we came out of them. I was so scared my knees were shaking."

C.T. Pedersen came from Oslo, Norway. He signed on the whaling ship the *Fearless* at the age of 14. That was the beginning of his illustrious career sailing the Arctic seas.

The famous Ice Pilot was good friends with Roald Amundsen, the great Norwegian polar explorer—the first man to navigate through the legendary Northwest Passage in 1905 and first to reach the South Pole in

*Teddy at the helm of the ship in stormy seas: "In the fall when we were whaling, gee, it was cold. That's when my dad would call from the crow's nest, 'Teddy, splice the main brace.' And I'd give each fellow a shot of rum."* (Pedersen Collection)

*"I never knew my dad until he took me out of the orphan home. The day he picked me up, a fellow came and gave me a little bag of sweets. Nobody told me where I was going. But they took me to the* Herman *and I knew my father was skipper."*

1911. It was Captain Pedersen who rescued Amundsen when the explorer's ship, the *Maud*, got trapped in the ice pack near Siberia.

"Amundsen wanted to drift over the North Pole. This was about 1920. He was several years in the ice, but he didn't get anywhere near the pole. The wind, ice, and currents were against him. He was drifting north of Siberia, when he finally fetched up on the Siberian coast around Cape Serdtse. Someone got word to my dad that Amundsen had no propeller. It was all banged up. So my dad sailed over and towed the *Maud* back to Nome.

"I met Amundsen later in Wainwright on the Alaska Arctic coast—the same year he attempted to fly over the North Pole in the early 1920s.

"Just to see him, you were rewarded. You felt it was an honor to know him. He was not one to get excited. He was a quiet man, calmly spoken. Every morning, he'd dip a bucket into the sea and have a drink of salt water. That was his tonic. He had a deep voice and he looked right at you. His eyes were serious. With that nose of his, it seemed to give him a lot of strength. He never talked of simple things. He never said anything, unless he had something to say. It felt good to be in his presence. He was kind and friendly and he liked his schnapps.

"But my dad now, he never drank. His family in Norway owned a livery stable—horses and wagons. When he was young, he drove the horses back and forth to the docks. He handled so many drunken sailors that he said he would never drink. And he never did.

"My dad was a self-made man," says Ted with admiration. "He couldn't read or write. But he taught himself mathematics and navigation. He studied the ice constantly. He could stay up in the crow's nest for days without sleep, watching, always watching for open leads in the ice and then snake his way through to open water. When he was just 20 years old, he was skipper of his own ship, a small schooner called the *Challenge*.

*"Just to see Amundsen, you were rewarded. You felt it was an honor to know him. He was not one to get excited. He was a quiet man, calmly spoken. Every morning, he'd dip a bucket into the sea and have a drink of salt water. That was his tonic. He had a deep voice and he looked right at you. His eyes were serious. With that nose of his, it seemed to give him a lot of strength. He never talked of simple things. He never said anything, unless he had something to say. He was kind and friendly and he liked his schnapps."*

Roald Amundsen, the first explorer to navigate through the legendary Northwest Passage in 1905 and the first to reach the South Pole in 1911.
(University of Alaska Fairbanks)

Above: *Captain C.T. Pedersen (left) and Roald Amundsen, the famous Norwegian polar explorer, were good friends. Here they are shown at Wainwright in 1922 before Amundsen's attempt to make the first polar flight. Captain Pedersen had towed Amundsen's ship, the* Maud, *from Siberia to Alaska in 1921 when the* Maud *had fetched up on the Siberian coast. Amundsen, the first man to reach the South Pole, had been attempting a drift across the North Pole. Wind, tides, ice, and currents were against him that year.*

Right: *Roald Amundsen's ship, the* Maud. *(Pedersen Collection)*

*Eskimo dancing at Pt. Hope, circa 1930. (Pedersen Collection)*

The *Elvira* was his next one. Then the *Herman*. Then the *Nanuk*. Then the *Patterson*.

"I was 11 when I went to sea. I spelled my name Peterson. That's the way they spelled it at the orphan home. But when I signed the ship's articles that way, my dad looked at it and said, 'Teddy, isn't my name good enough for you?'

"You see," relates Ted laughing, "I made a Swede out of myself, instead of a Norwegian.

"Every year, we made a round trip between San Francisco and the Arctic. (A journey of about 17,000 miles.) From San Francisco, we'd sail to Dutch

*Eskimos at Pt. Hope on the Arctic Ocean in the 1930s when Ted was on board the* Patterson.
*(Pedersen Collection)*

*"I think of my dad so often. Sometimes I dream of him. I feel like we're in contact. Every once in a while, I can hear him. He used to sing when he was jolly. I can just hear him calling, 'Teddy, Teddy . . .' The Eskimos couldn't say 'Teddy.' They'd say, 'Tetty, oh Tetty, you big boy.'"*

"One trip we got 60,000 fox skins!" says Ted, shown here loaded with fur. "Fur didn't take up any room. You could put 100 furs in a little bag." (Pedersen Collection)

Harbor in the Aleutians. Then on to St. Lawrence Island, King's Island, Cape Prince of Wales, and Nome. Then we'd travel the coast until Barrow, go east of Barrow to Herschel Island and then on to Banks Island in the Canadian Northwest Territories. All that territory we were trading. After we were through trading, we'd go after whales. We'd sail back towards Wrangel Island and whale along the ice pack until October and then head for San Francisco.

"Wrangel Island in the Arctic Ocean is now in Soviet territory, but it wasn't then. It was a great place for polar bear, whale, seal, and walrus . . . ohhh . . . thousands of walrus in the summer. You could hear them in the fog just bellowing away.

"In 1916, my father put three Eskimo families from the village of Pt. Hope on shore at Banks Island to trap for him. Because of the ice conditions, we couldn't pick them up for three years. When we brought them on board in 1919, boy, were they loaded with fur! Polar bear, seal, and foxes. Sack after sack of fox skins came on board.

"We went north with the ship's hold full of trade goods— hardtack, sugar, coffee, tea, flour, rice, traps, guns, cases of ammunition, tools, calico, thread, skin needles, skinning knives, axes, eggs preserved in salt, matches, things like that. Twenty hardtack equaled one hair seal skin. A polar bear skin was about seven dollars a foot, top price. Everything was trade goods. No cash. The Eskimos had no money. The only time we got cash was if there was a white trapper.

"In those days, the Eskimo women were well tattooed. The men cut a ring of hair around their heads and the old-timers wore lip labarets, an ivory decoration which fit through a hole in their lip. On St. Lawrence Island, they smoked long Chinese brass pipes and they still wore loon-skin parkas. That's the way it was in 1916.

"One trip we got 60,000 white fox skins! My father was dealing with H. Liebes Company in Frisco. That was a big furrier. The most valuable fur then was a black or a silver fox. Dad would pay as much as $300 for a silver fox. But white fox was worth only about $12.

"We got hundreds of polar bears. We even brought back live polar bear. Every year, we'd catch two or three cubs and feed

*"We got hundreds of polar bears. We even brought back live polar bear. Every year, we'd catch two or three cubs and feed them milk. We sold them to the Barnum and Bailey Circus. The last two we brought down here were for Mr. Hearst at San Simeon Castle on the coast of California."*

*(Pedersen Collection)*

(Pedersen Collection)

them milk. We sold them to the Barnum and Bailey Circus. The last two we brought down were for Mr. Hearst at San Simeon Castle on the coast of California. Fur didn't take up any room. You could put 100 furs in a little bag. We carried 400 tons of cargo—trade goods and food-stuffs—on the way up. On the way back, we'd carry furs, baleen (whalebone), and whale oil. We rendered the whale right out there on ship, stripped it like peeling an apple, then boiled down the blubber to oil. Each whale was worth about $10,000. The oil was used for soap and tanning leather.

"The bowhead whale is exclusively an Arctic whale and it ranges along the rim of the Arctic ice pack. The whale measures about 75 feet long so it is rather gigantic game to hunt in a 28-foot whaleboat.

"In the fall when we were whaling, gee, it was cold.

"That's when my dad would call from the crow's nest, 'Teddy, splice the main brace.' And I'd get this big pitcher with half rum and half water and give each fellow in the whaleboat a shot of rum, whether they'd gotten a whale or not. I remember this one old Portagee on board—he liked his drink so well. He'd swallow the rum. Then he'd rattle the glass between his teeth to get the last drop," says Ted, chuckling at the memory.

"Up in the crow's nest, you could see the spout of a whale before the boats did. In those days, I'd take coffee up to my dad. I'd climb the rope steps, 130 feet up the ratlines. At first I was slow, because I was a little nervous. But pretty soon, I was sliding down the halyards. One time, I remember, the boats were just coming up to this whale. My father whispered, 'Just one more spout.' And then he yelled, 'There she white waters!'

"When the men in the whaleboat struck the whale, it made quite a commotion.

"If the sail came down, my father knew the boat was connected to the whale. Then he'd holler, 'Fast boat!' so the skeleton crew down below would know. Fast boat meant it was fast to the whale. Then the whale tows the boat around until it tires out. That's what they used to call a 'Nantucket Sleigh Ride' after all the New England Yankee whalers.

"If you spotted a whale, you hollered, 'Blooooooooow.' And if they caught that whale, you'd get 10 dollars.

"When the mate would yell, 'Blooooooow,' the Old Man (another term for the captain) would go to the crow's nest and relieve the mate. He'd watch the whale to see if it was feeding or traveling. If traveling, you couldn't catch it. But if the whale was feeding, he'd sing out to the mate, 'Call all hands.' And the crew would come out on the quarterdeck and stand by the boat.

"'Lower away when you're ready!' my dad would yell. And that was it.

"There were no commands on the whale boat. It was very quiet. A bowhead whale is so sensitive. If you're sailing along and knock the boat or the sail jibes and makes a noise, boy, the next time you see that whale, he's spouting high and way up to the windward. They really know. That's what you call 'gallying a whale.' If you gally a whale, you might as well forget it.

"The only time there's talking is when you strike the whale and the mate yells, 'Give it to him!'

"The harpoon is fastened to 300 fathoms of line neatly coiled in the tub. It's laid in just perfect, not a kink. You don't get foul of the line. When it goes out, it goes so fast that the fellow in the stern throws water on the loggerhead to keep it from burning. When the whale stops running, you take a turn in the

*"Up in the crow's nest, you could see the spout of a whale before the boats did. In those days, I'd take coffee up to my dad. I'd climb the rope steps, 130 feet up the ratlines. At first I was slow, because I was a little nervous. But pretty soon, I was sliding down the halyards. One time, I remember, the boats were just coming up to this whale. My father whispered, 'Just one more spout.' And then he yelled, "There she white waters!"*

*The* Nanuk. *(Pedersen Collection)*

line. When he comes up, you pull in all the slack. You play him just like a fish until he tires out and you get right up to him. Then you shoot him with a shoulder gun. If anything fouls up, you have an axe up front in the boat so you can chop the line, because the whale could tow you under."

The first time Teddy went out in a whaleboat, he was thrilled. He wanted to be the harpooner, but the mate said, "Your father would give me hell if I let you." He was only 14. Watching many times from the crow's nest of the big ship with his father, Teddy thought it all looked grand.

"But when that whale sur-

Above: *Ted, 1927, in the Lighthouse Service.*
Right: *Seal rookery, three miles south of Cape Sarichef in the Aleutians.* (Pedersen Collection)

In the late 1920s, Ted was keeper of the farthest west lighthouse in America. It was situated on Unimak Island, one of the Aleutian Islands, which stretch 1,000 miles from mainland Alaska towards the heart of Siberia. *(Pedersen Collection)*

*"My front yard was the Bering Sea and in my backyard were four volcanoes and the Pacific Ocean. It's one of the foggiest and stormiest places in the world. Sailors called that place 'the graveyard of the Pacific.'"*

*"The whale rose up and flipped over, tossing the boat up in the air. Everyone else was thrown clear, but I was trapped under the boat."*

faced right in front of us, oooooooohhh, my heart nearly stopped.

"I was hoping we wouldn't get near it. And here, that's what we were supposed to do," Teddy laughs. "I was so scared. It looked like the bottom of the ocean coming up. He let out a whoosh of air with a very loud noise. The wind was blowing our direction and the smell was horrible. About the third spout, the mate, who was right behind me, yelled 'Give it to him!' Gee, I nearly jumped off that thwart.

"Once, I was in a whaleboat that upset.

"The mate was already fast to a whale and we happened to come alongside him. The whale was going pretty slowly. The second mate—his name was Mr. Lee—decided that he was going to put another harpoon in him. He came on the whale at the wrong angle. Instead of sideways, he went over the back of the whale.

"The whale rose up and flipped over, tossing the boat up

*Ted, bear hunting on Unimak Island in the 1920s. (Pedersen Collection)*

in the air. Everyone else was thrown clear, but I was trapped under the boat.

"I couldn't swim a stroke.

"I managed to crawl out from underneath and get on top of the boat. Here were the three Eskimos. Their feet were in the air and their heads were down in the water. I saw Mr. Lee's head pop up, and boy, his face was blue. He had gotten foul with the line and gone down. Before he got himself free, his face turned bright blue. He was about

*Duck hunting on Kodiak Island.* (Pedersen Collection)

50 feet from the boat. I could see the line was still foul with the boat. So I reached down, grabbed it, and pulled it up.

"'Come on, Mr. Lee,' I yelled. And he came hand over hand to the boat. The mate knew how to swim, but the Eskimos didn't and I didn't. That boat went over so fast, I hardly even knew what happened. The chief mate's boat came over and picked up the Eskimos and then picked us up and towed us in."

One year, Captain C.T. Pedersen met a nurse at Point Barrow. As Teddy describes it, "She was 20 years younger than he was and a bossy sort of thing. She decided she wasn't going to stay in Pt. Barrow. So we took her out whaling. My dad was teaching me navigation and I had even learned arithmetic. She would sit there on the couch in his cabin all primmed up in her white nurse's uniform. Anyway, my dad sort of took a liking to her. When we got to Frisco, my dad asked me if it was all right if he married her. That's how I happened to leave. She sent me to Mount Hermon School in Massachusetts. It was in 1921. I was 16.

"In those days, I knew nothing but cuss words and I smoked. Mount Hermon was a religious school. I didn't last very

(Pedersen Collection)

long there. But going to Mount Hermon was the making of me. Putting my thoughts down on paper really got to me. I just took a liking to it. I said, 'Someday I'm going to write a story.'

"When I talk about the past, it's all in my mind. I haven't forgotten anything, honestly, all the characters I've been with, the real old-timers.

"I think of my dad so often. Sometimes I dream of him. I feel like we're in contact. Every once in a while, I can hear him. He used to sing when he was jolly. I can just hear him calling, 'Teddy, Teddy . . .' The Eskimos couldn't say 'Teddy.' They'd say, 'Tetty, oh Tetty, you big boy.'"

The last year Teddy sailed

with his father was in 1935. That was the year the Old Man was going to retire and let Ted be the next captain of the *Patterson*. But in 1936, the bottom dropped out of the fur market. So they were forced to sell out to the Hudson's Bay Company. By that time, Ted had already spent seven years in the Lighthouse Service. The rest of his life he

*His eyes are distant. And in the flickering shadows beyond the poetry, one has the feeling that somewhere out of the past a jolly voice is calling "Teddy, Teddy," the wind is blowing, and the halyards are beating against the mast.*

would spend navigating and piloting mail boats, ships, and tankers for the U.S. Postal Service, the oil companies, fish canneries, Japanese cargo firms, and filmmakers.

As pilot on Jacques Cousteau's exploration vessel the *Calypso* while it was in Alaska waters, Ted piloted the French scientist and marine crusader from Anchorage south to Homer while the crew shot footage of killer whales. While sailing, Ted recited poetry learned during those long, lonely years out at Cape Sarichef in the lighthouse. A favorite is Robert Service's "The Spell of the Yukon."

As the *Calypso* sailed into Kachemak Bay and towards Ted's home in Bear Cove, one of the Frenchmen asked him in a quote from the poem, "Are those where your pearly peaks are gleaming?"

In the summer evening, Teddy retells this story for his kayaking friends. The sun has set. Only the warm, soft, yellow light of candles illuminates the darkness. His voice booms out "The Spell of the Yukon" and then cracks with a kind of raspiness. There is a tear running down his cheek. Softly, he repeats the lines, whispering:

*I've watched the big, husky sun wallow,*
*In crimson and gold, and grow dim,*
*Till the moon set the pearly peaks gleaming,*
*And the stars tumbled out, neck and crop;*
*And I've thought that I surely was dreaming,*
*With the peace o' the world piled on top.*

His eyes are distant. And in the flickering shadows beyond the poetry, one has the feeling that somewhere out of the past a jolly voice is calling, "Teddy, Teddy," the wind is blowing, and the halyards are beating against the mast.

Above: *"Fast Eddie" Fortier is the last living spy from World War II in Alaska. This photo was taken in Anchorage in 1989.* (Nan Elliot)

Left: *Spy of yesteryear, Ed Fortier in 1944 was an undercover agent on the island of Shemya at the far end of the Aleutian Chain.* (Fortier Collection)

# A Special Thanks

First, I would like to thank Jürgen Boden, president of the publishing company Alouette Verlag in Hamburg, West Germany, for the inspiration years ago that led to the creation of this book. For those who are interested, Alouette Verlag is publishing a co-edition of this book in German.

In addition to the wonderful hospitality, time, and friendship I shared with the characters featured between the covers of this book, several others have been most generous in helping this project to its conclusion.

David Rychetnik, an extremely talented filmmaker and graphic designer, got me launched on his computer system and was always there to bail me out when the computers and I misspoke. He was also very free, as always, with his illuminating advice and his time.

My friends at Connections Ltd.—Randy Johnson, Gary Lamar, Steve Rychetnik, and Kathy Dunn—were kind enough to let me camp out for weeks in their office, use their equipment, and keep me entertained with their delightful humor.

Scottie Hurlbert, a wacky computer whiz kid from bush Alaska with a golden heart, made magic electronic connections between computers and files, which I never understood but which, bless his soul, worked!

Wanda Seamster, famous artist and graphic designer at the

University of Alaska's Arctic Environmental Information and Data Center, not only created the map for the book, but spent hours—liberally laced with her wit and humor—advising me on design.

The photographers who helped me out are all very talented Alaskans, most of whom live pretty wild lives themselves: Ted Bell, Joel Bennett, Rob Stapleton, Dennis Hellawell, Mark Kelley, Bill Hess, Nancy Simmerman, and Jeff Schultz.

*Anchorage Daily News* photographers Fran Durner, Paul Brown, Bob Hallinen, and Erik Hill filled in some of the important missing links. Thanks to their editors—Howard Weaver, Mike Campbell, and Richard Murphy—for permission to run these photos. For his darkroom work, fortitude, and "good eye," a special thanks to Dan Smith of the *Daily News*. Also many thanks to Robert Atwood, publisher of the *Anchorage Times*, for use of historical photos from the *Times*.

I am particularly grateful, too, for the use of photographs from the National Park Service, the United States Navy, the University of Alaska Fairbanks, and the Anchorage Museum of History and Art.

Finally, a special hats off to members of the clan who have been great cheerleaders and I adore them for their laughter, love, and encouragement—in particular Enock, Rick, John Clephan (alias "His Lordship"), Little Laurie, Clif, Bette Harvey, Tara, Stefan, Geza, Auntie M, and all the Kings.

\*　　　\*　　　\*

Last, but certainly not least, is my old friend "Fast Eddie" Fortier, the classic image of a sourdough Alaskan with his wonderful white hair, salty language, and (he'll deny it) marshmallow heart. He promised to read my manuscript and he did, giving me a blow-by-blow critique. The editor of *Alaska Magazine* for many, many years and writer for the *National Observer*, Ed Fortier is also the last living spy from World War II in Alaska.

"I wasn't a goddamn spy, Nannie," he always corrects me, "I was in counter-espionage."

Call it what you like—secret agent, G-2 man, military intelligence—a spy is a spy. Ed had

*"You're setting me up, baby. And I've been set up by some pretty tricky women in my time."*
*—Fast Eddie*

such a fantastic photographic memory that as soon as he got to Alaska in 1942, they shoved him right under cover. If pressed, he'll grudgingly admit he was a "damn good agent."

Fast Eddie is a marvelously volatile mixture of French, Irish, and Italian. His language is peppered with colorful expletives, which makes it all the funnier because he is also a devout Roman Catholic and constantly apologizes for swearing. Pious as he is, he'll never forgive me—"a goddamn Protestant"—for meeting Mother Teresa. He'll also never forgive me for putting him in this book.

I wanted to feature him in a chapter of his own, but every time I'd start jotting down notes or flip my tape recorder on, he'd narrow his eyes and growl, "You're setting me up, baby. And I've been set up by some pretty tricky women in my time."

Hate to say this, Ed, but you lost this round. You've been set up again. And I won.
*—Nan Elliot*